I am grateful to God for everything! And I believe that the meaning of life is to give meaning to other lives. Laura and Alice, you are the meaning of my life.

When we stimulate our children with cognitive exercises, we are enhancing their future."

Stimulating children with cognitive exercises is important because it helps them develop their mental skills. Cognitive exercises are activities that challenge the child's thinking, memory, attention, problem-solving, and language skills.

When cutting out the figures to assemble, use blunt scissors and ask for an adult's help.

Leonardo Macedo

2024

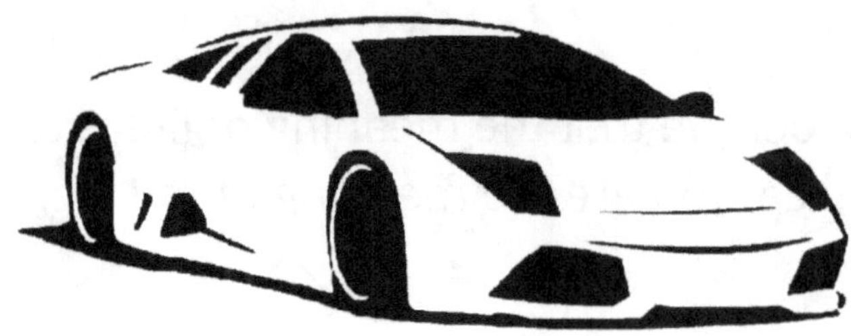
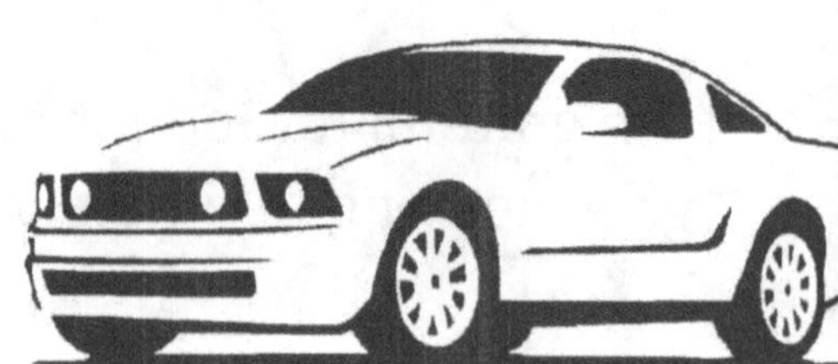

This Book Belongs to:

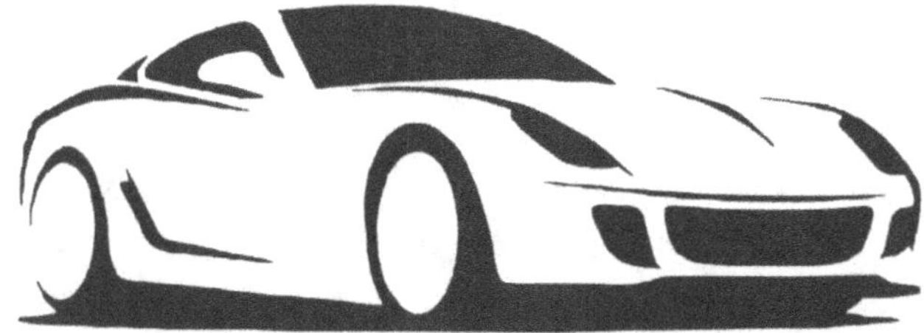
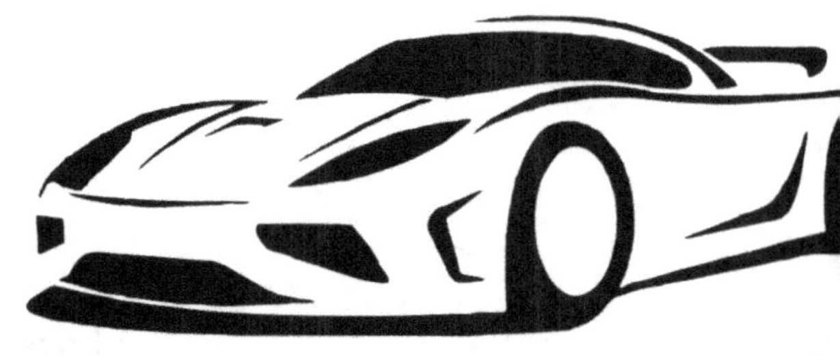
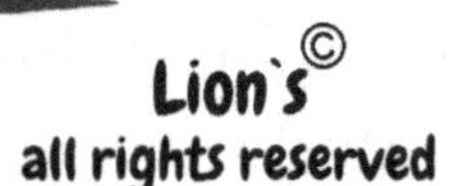

Lion`s ©
all rights reserved

ALL RIGHTS RESERVED©
2024

No part of this publication may be reproduced, distributed, or transmitted in any form or by any means, including photocopying, recording, or other electronic or mechanical methods, without the prior written permission of the publisher, except for brief quotations incorporated in critical reviews and other specific noncommercial uses. Any unauthorized replica of this work is prohibited.

Lion`s©
publications

Test Color Page

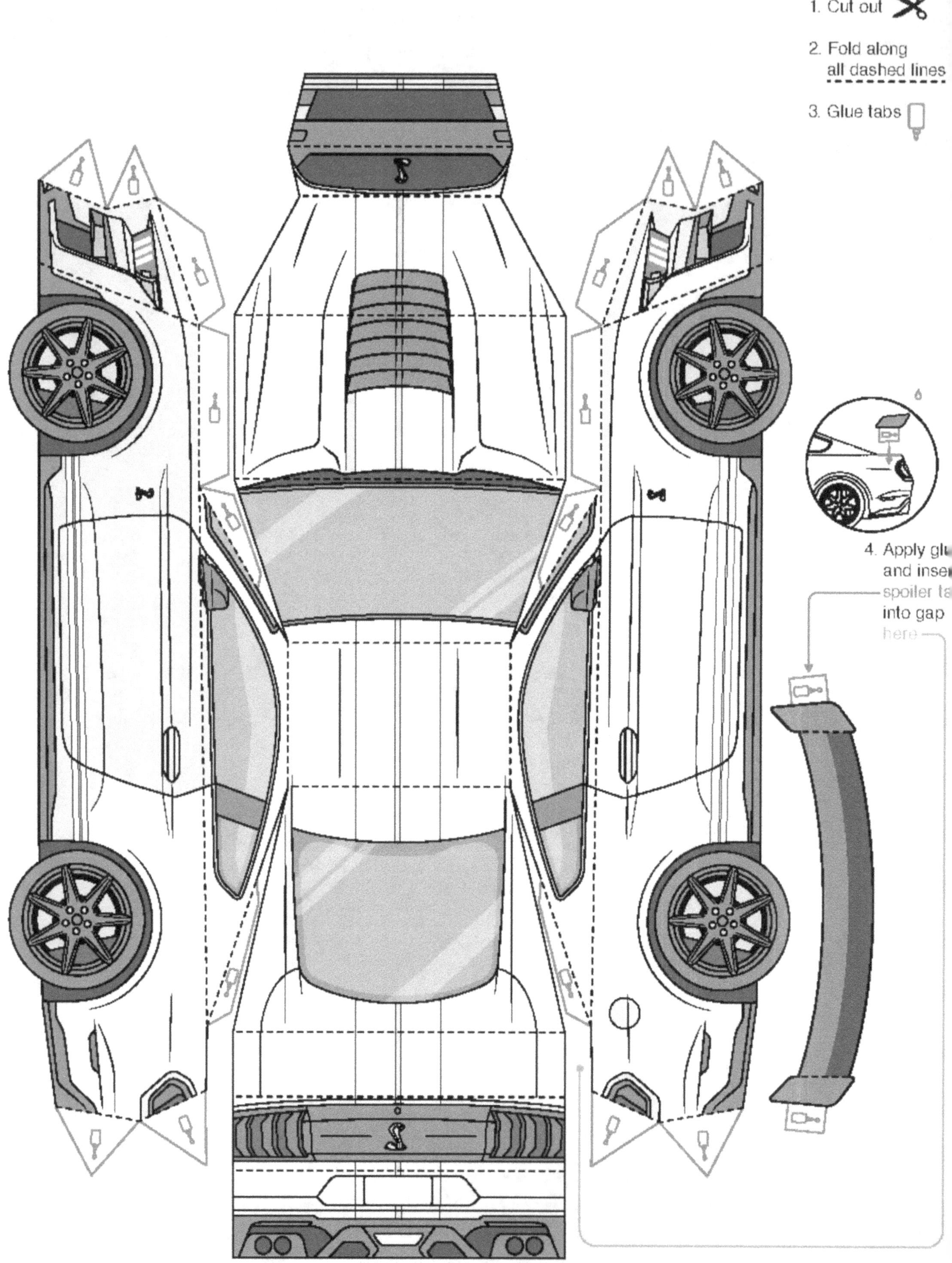

1. Cut out
2. Fold along all dashed lines
3. Glue tabs
4. Apply glue and insert spoiler tab into gap here

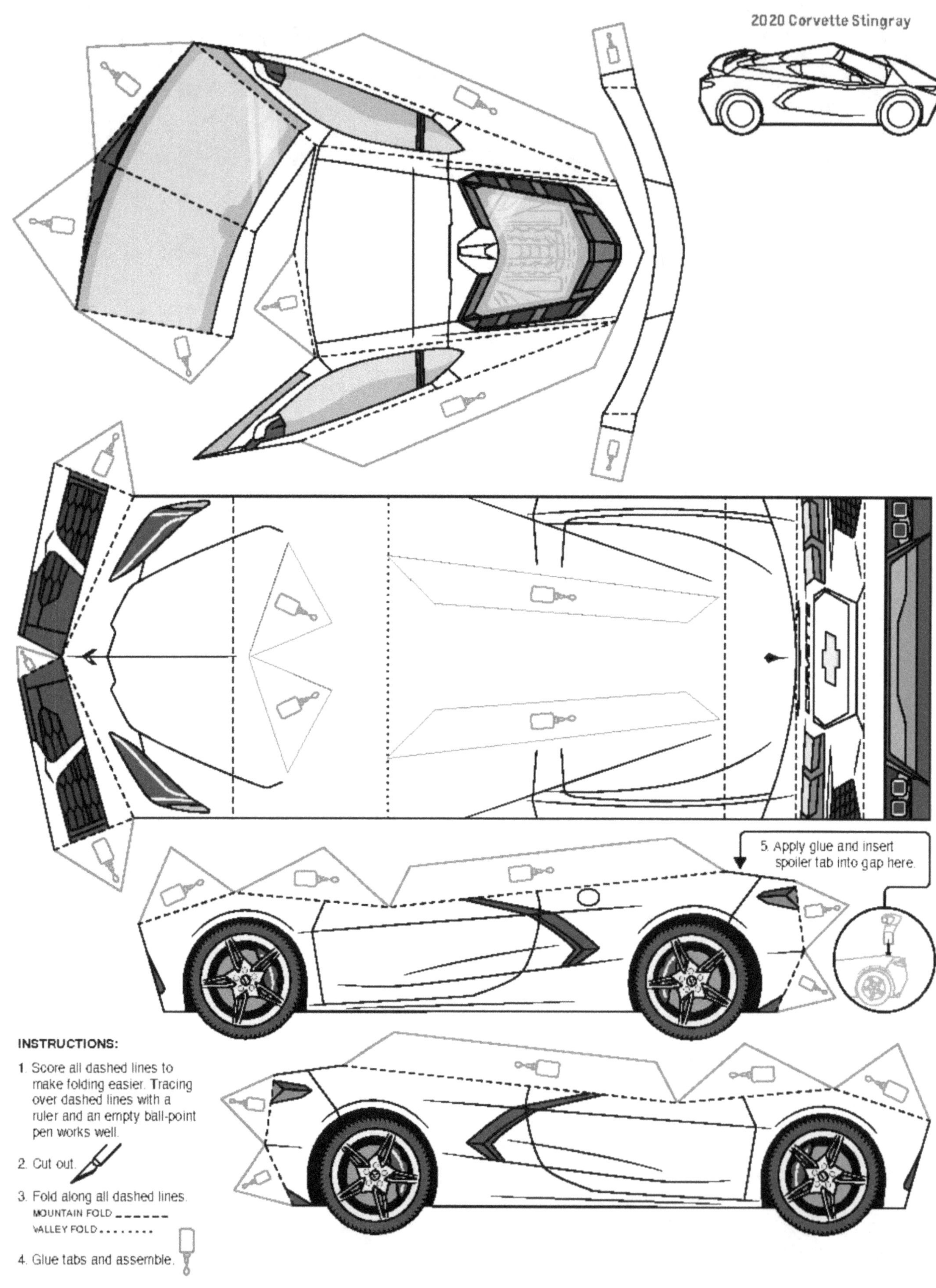

2020 Corvette Stingray
5. Apply glue and insert spoiler tab into gap here.
INSTRUCTIONS:
1. Score all dashed lines to make folding easier. Tracing over dashed lines with a ruler and an empty ball-point pen works well.
2. Cut out.
3. Fold along all dashed lines.
MOUNTAIN FOLD
VALLEY FOLD
4. Glue tabs and assemble.

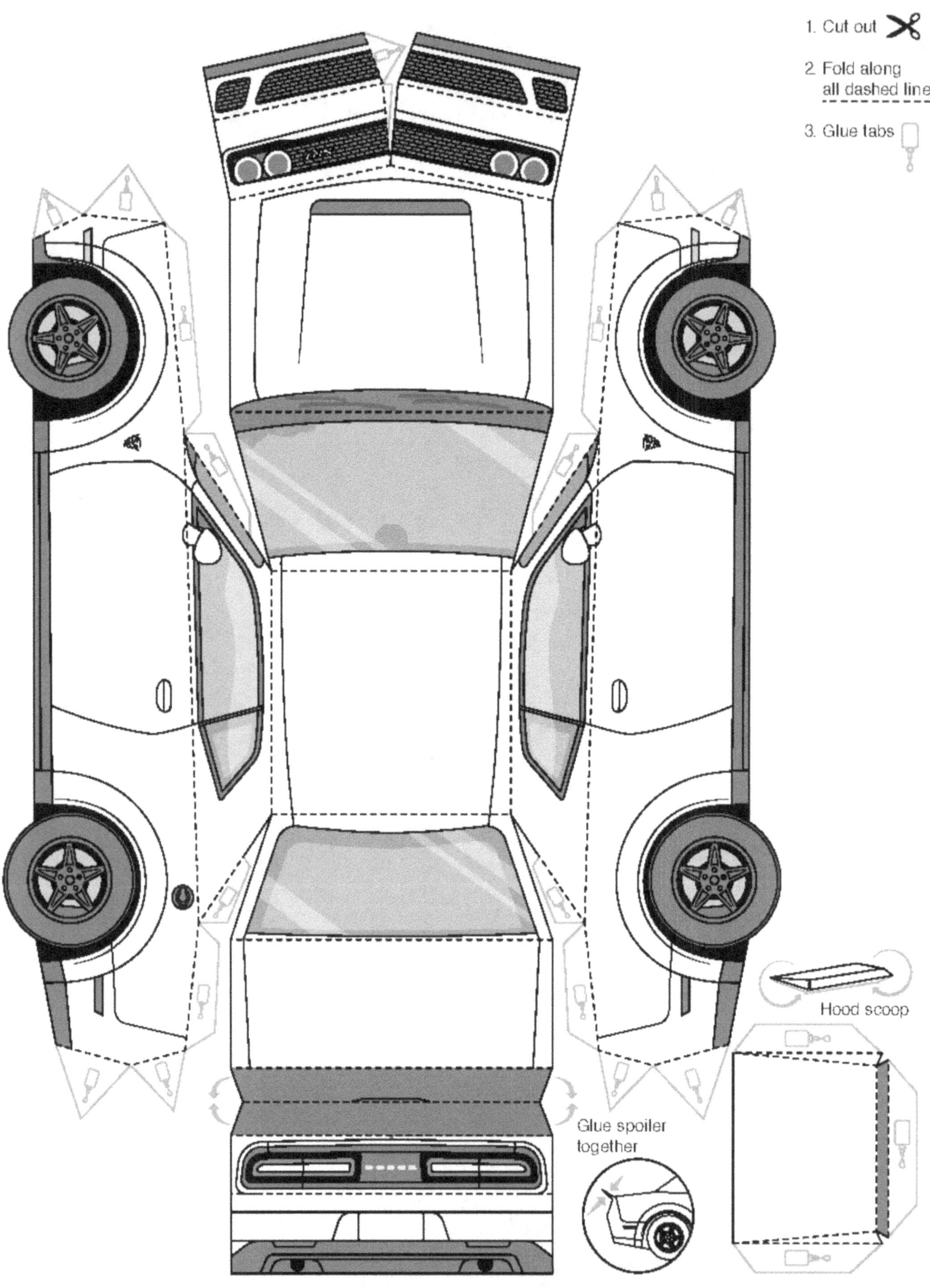

1. Cut out
2. Fold along all dashed lines
3. Glue tabs
Hood scoop
Glue spoiler together

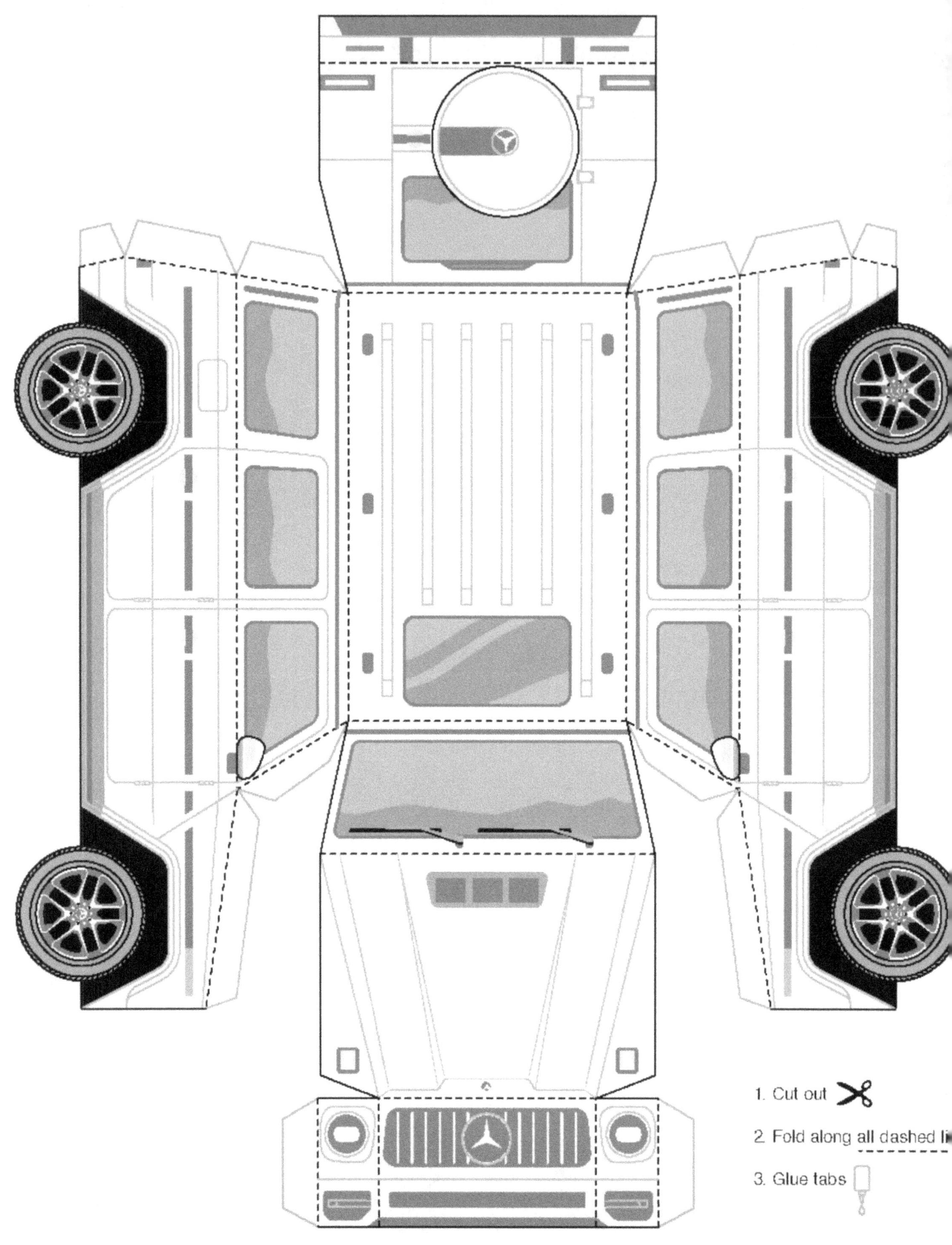

1. Cut out
2. Fold along all dashed li
3. Glue tabs

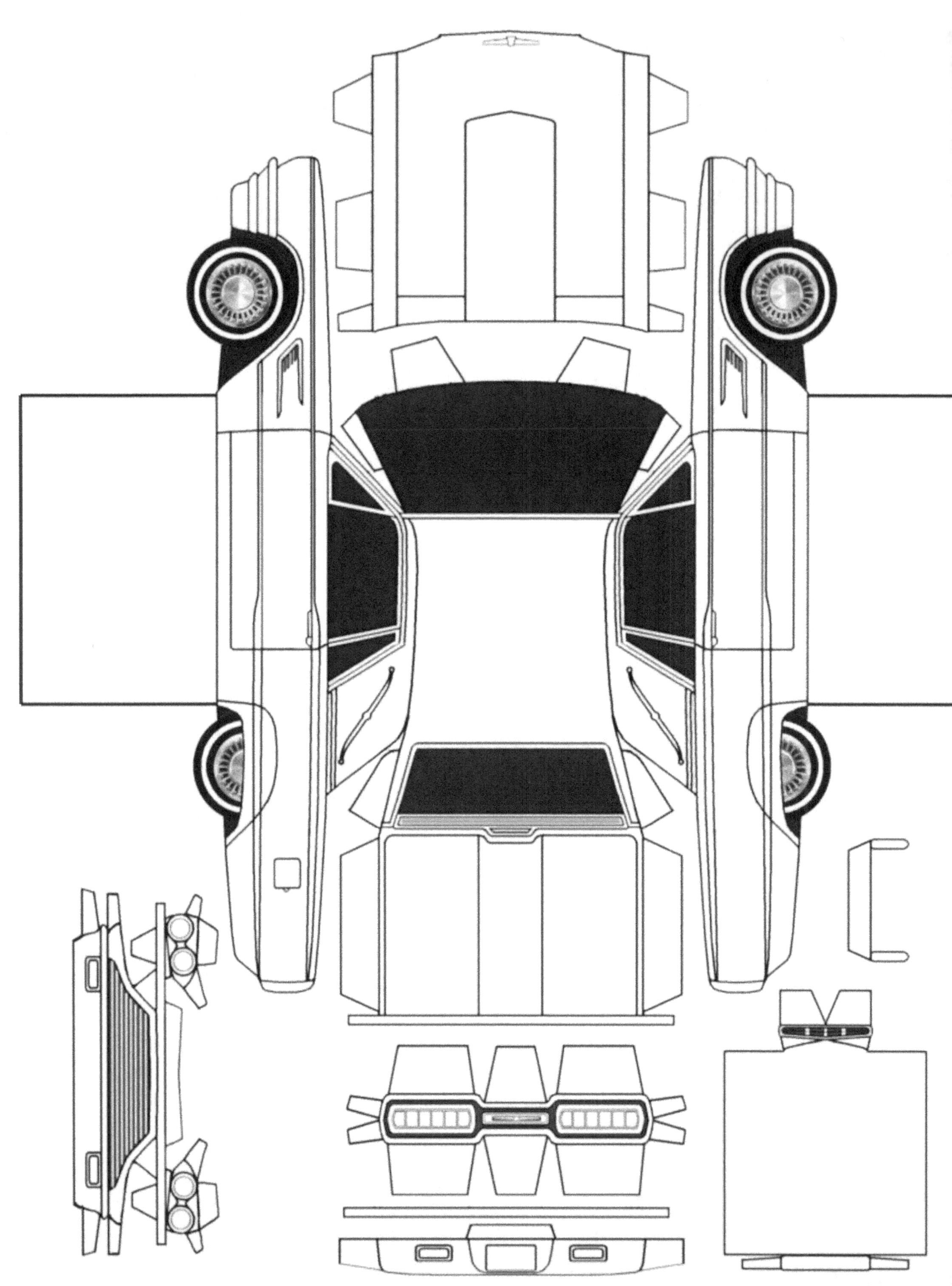

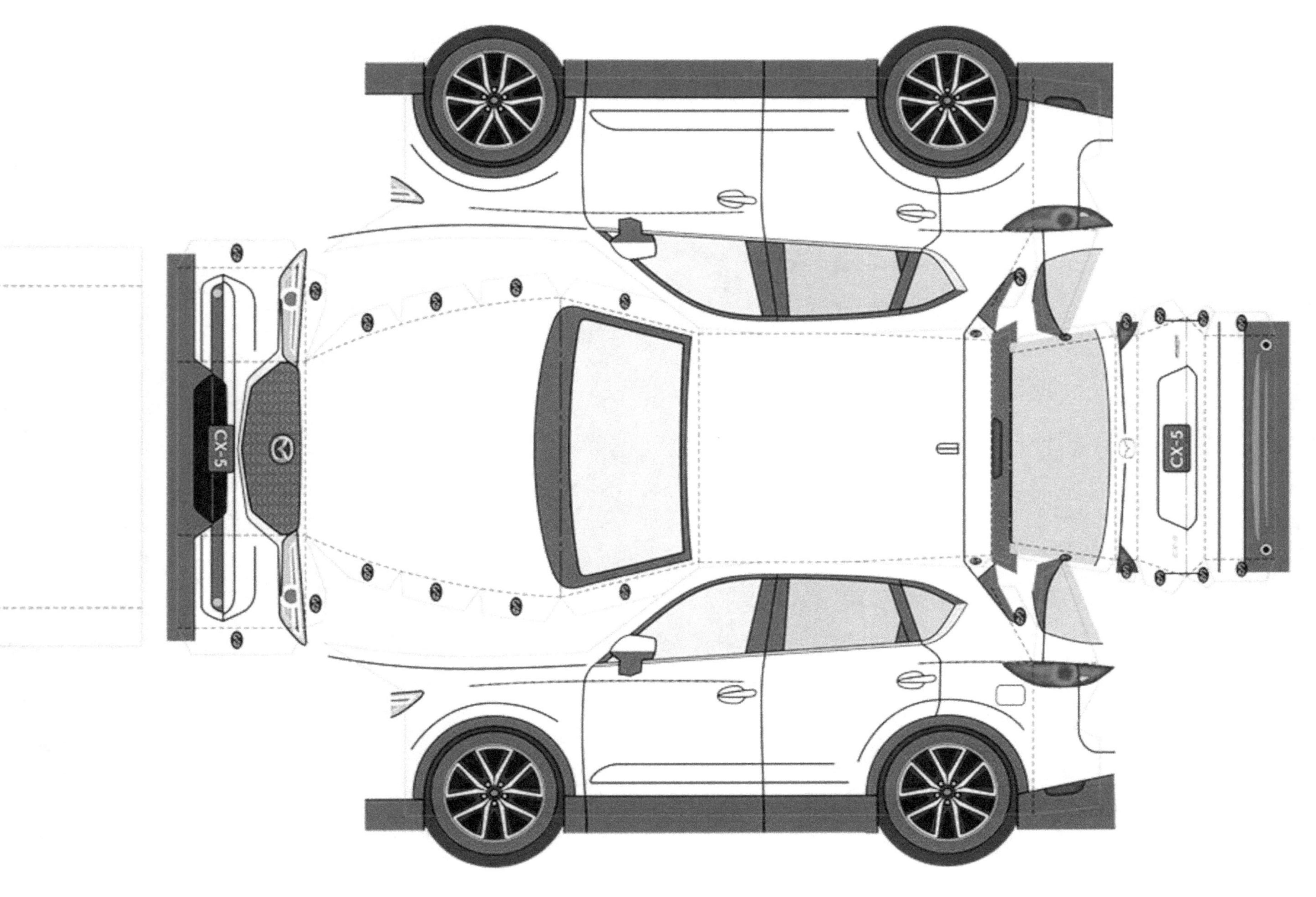
CX-5
CX-5

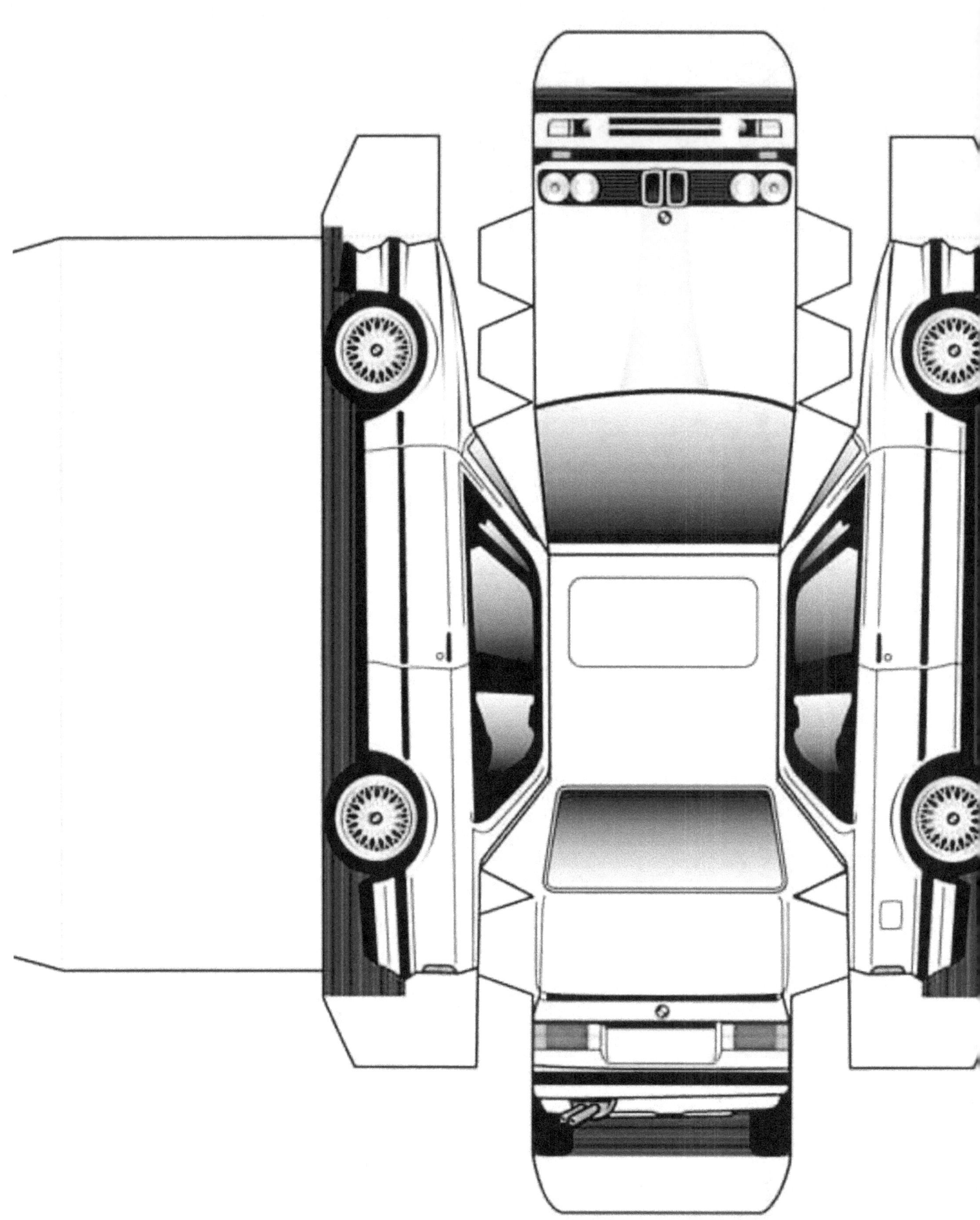

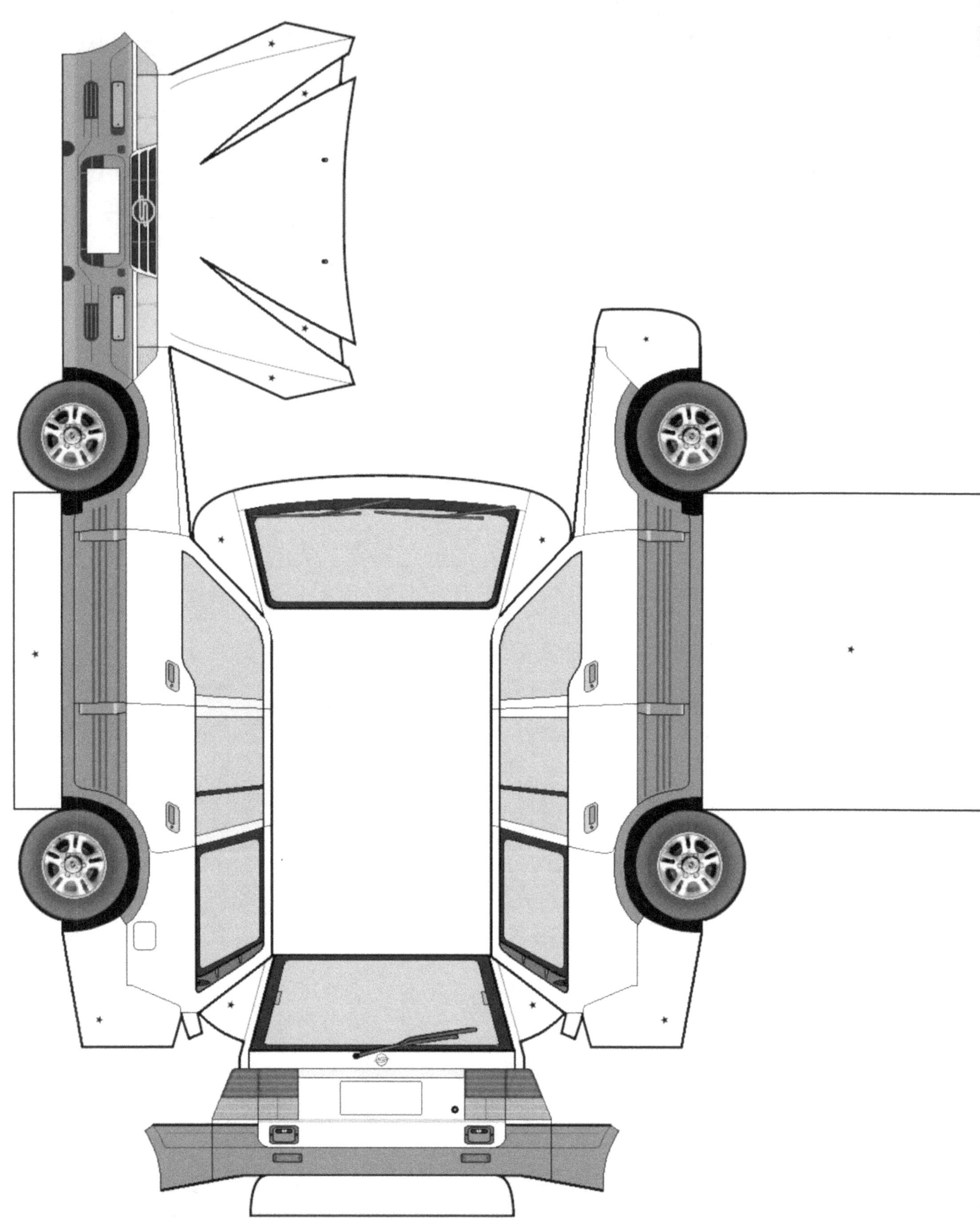

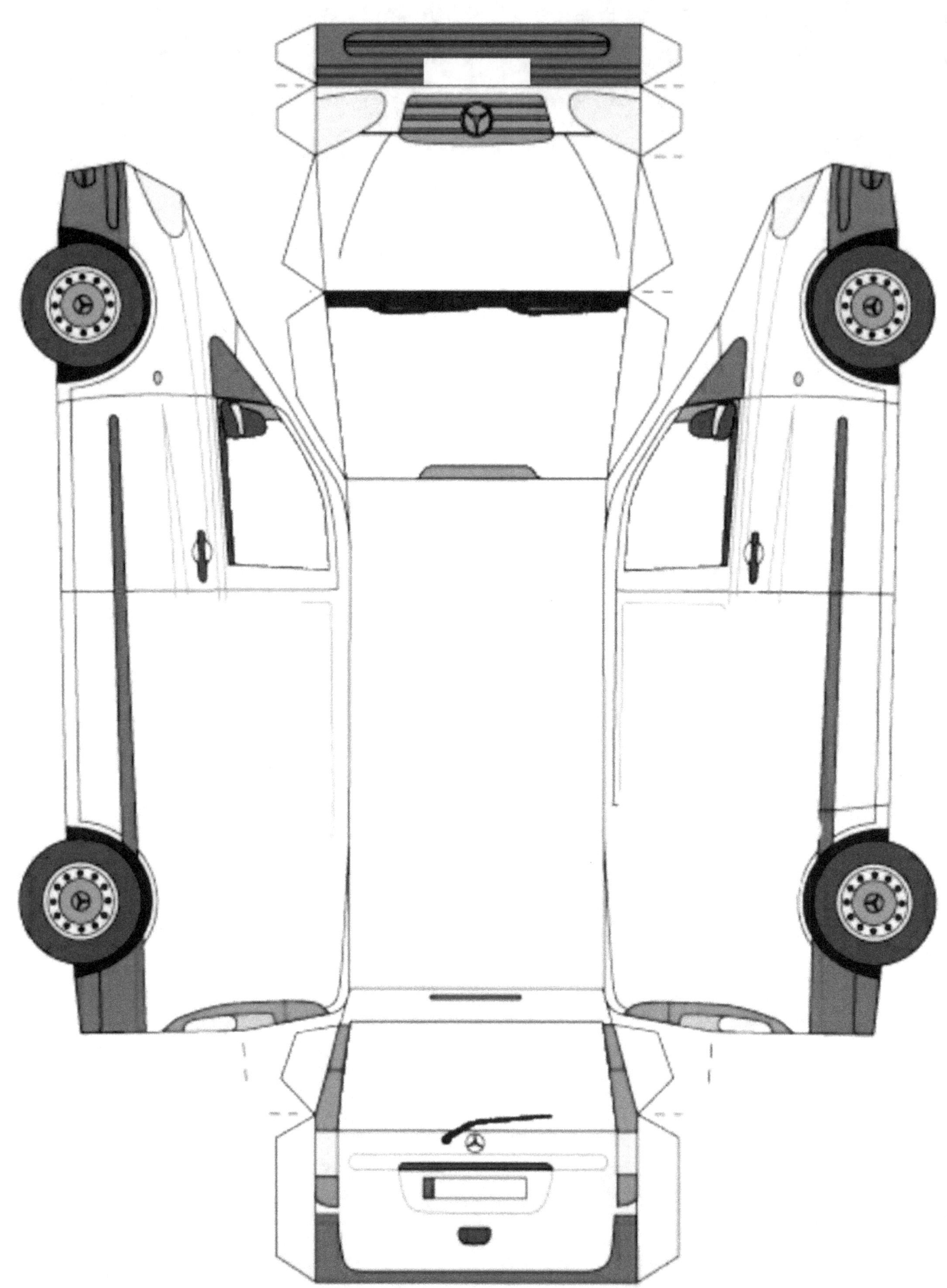

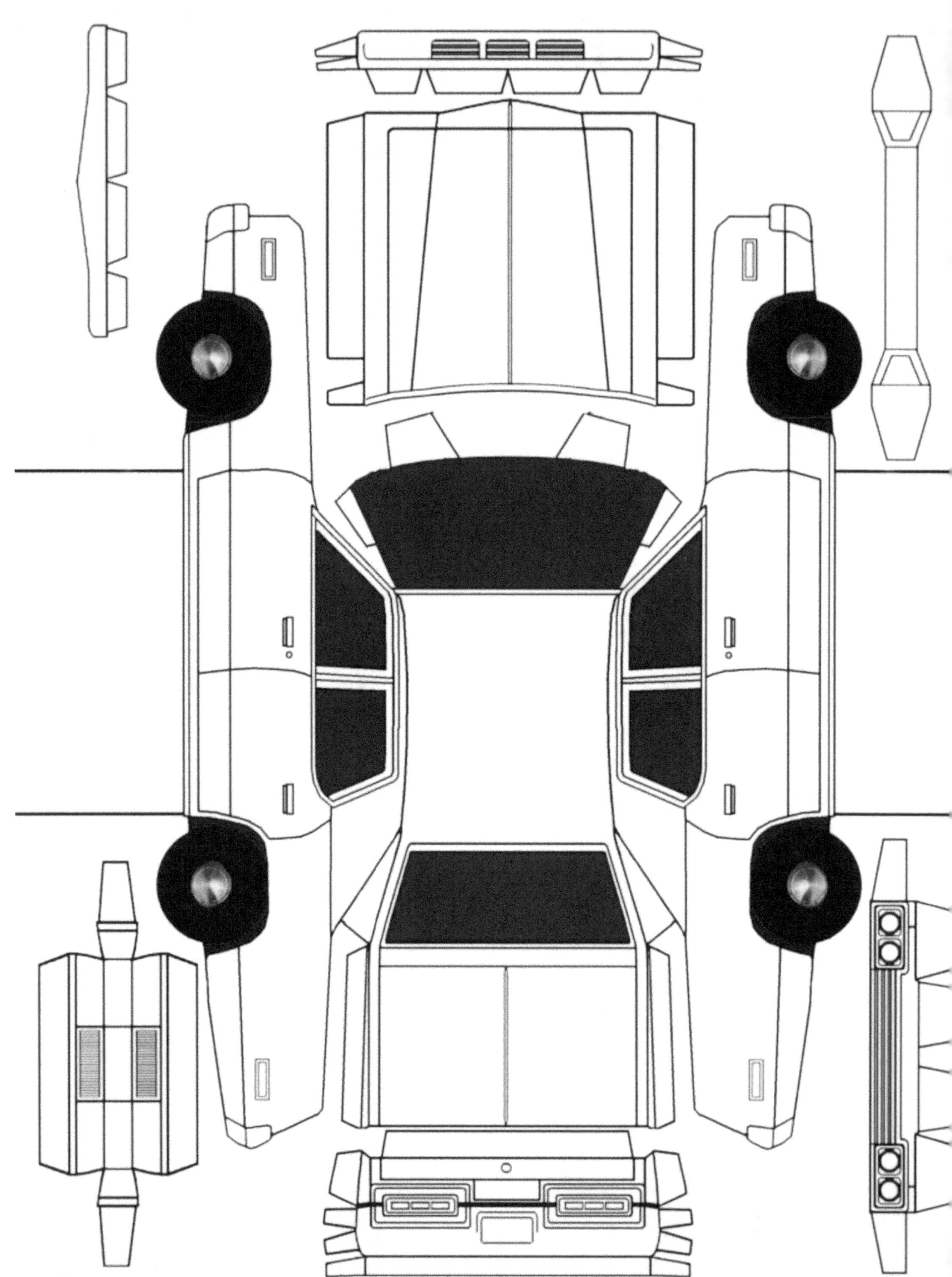

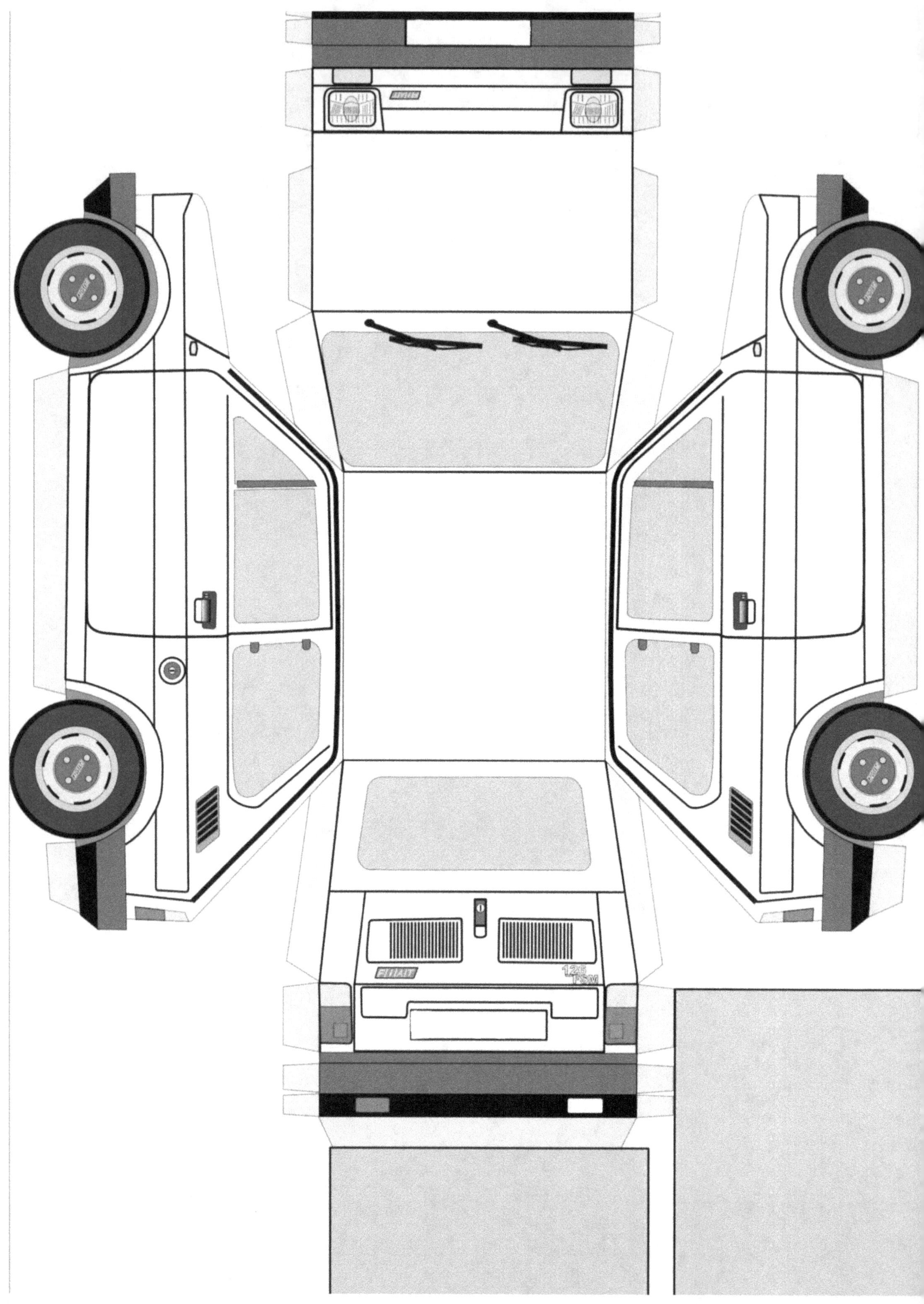

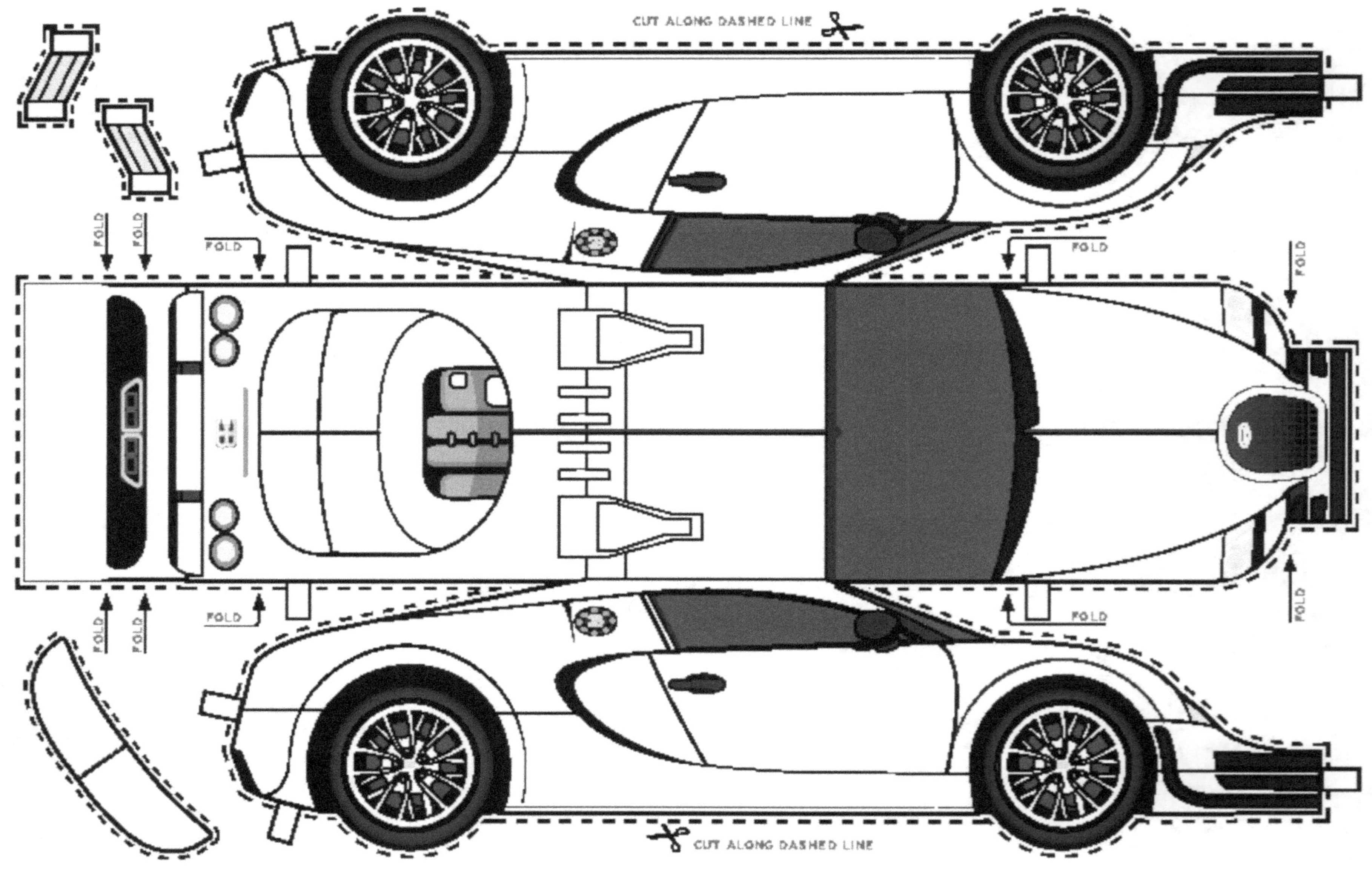

CUT ALONG DASHED LINE
CUT ALONG DASHED LINE
FOLD
FOLD
FOLD
FOLD
FOLD
FOLD
FOLD
FOLD

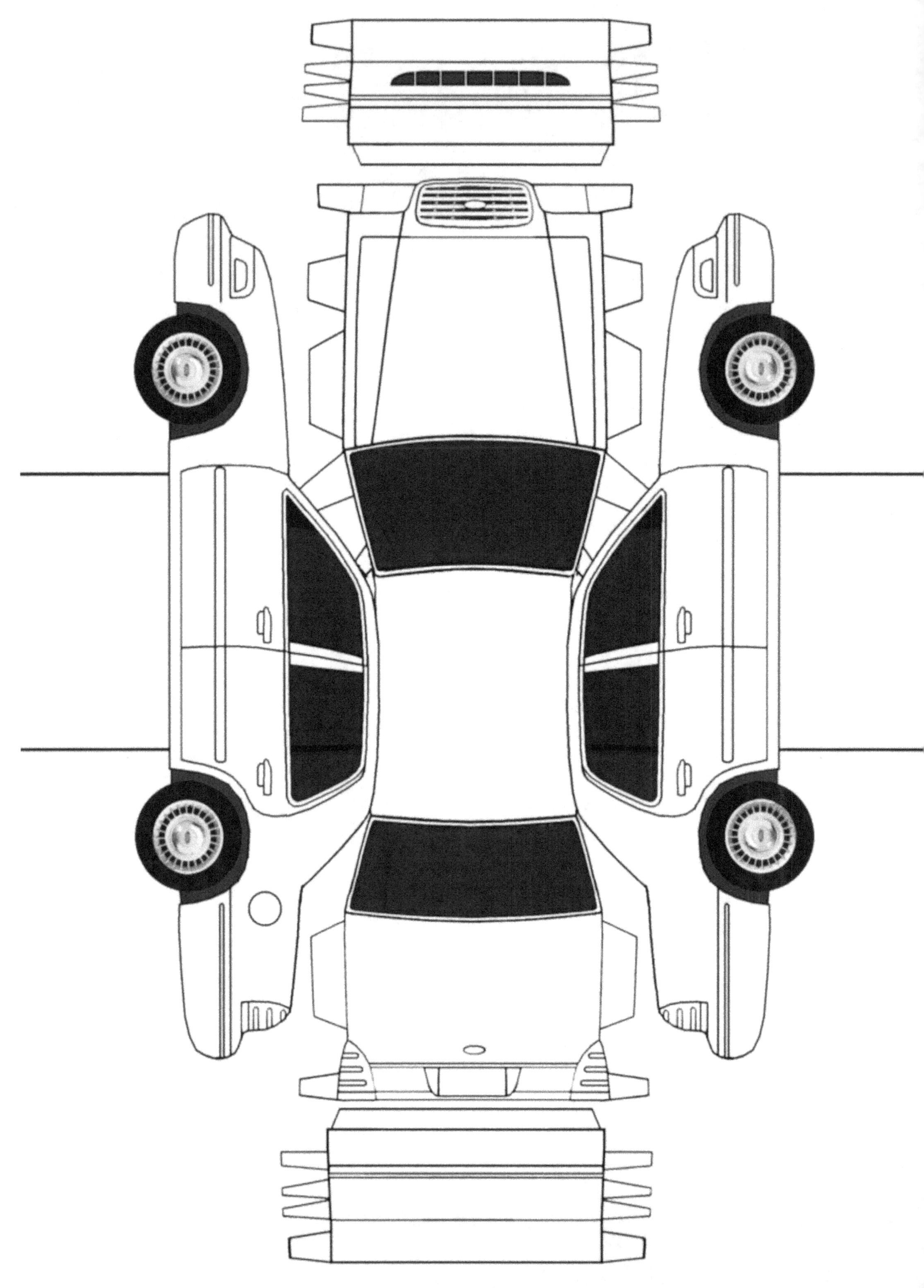

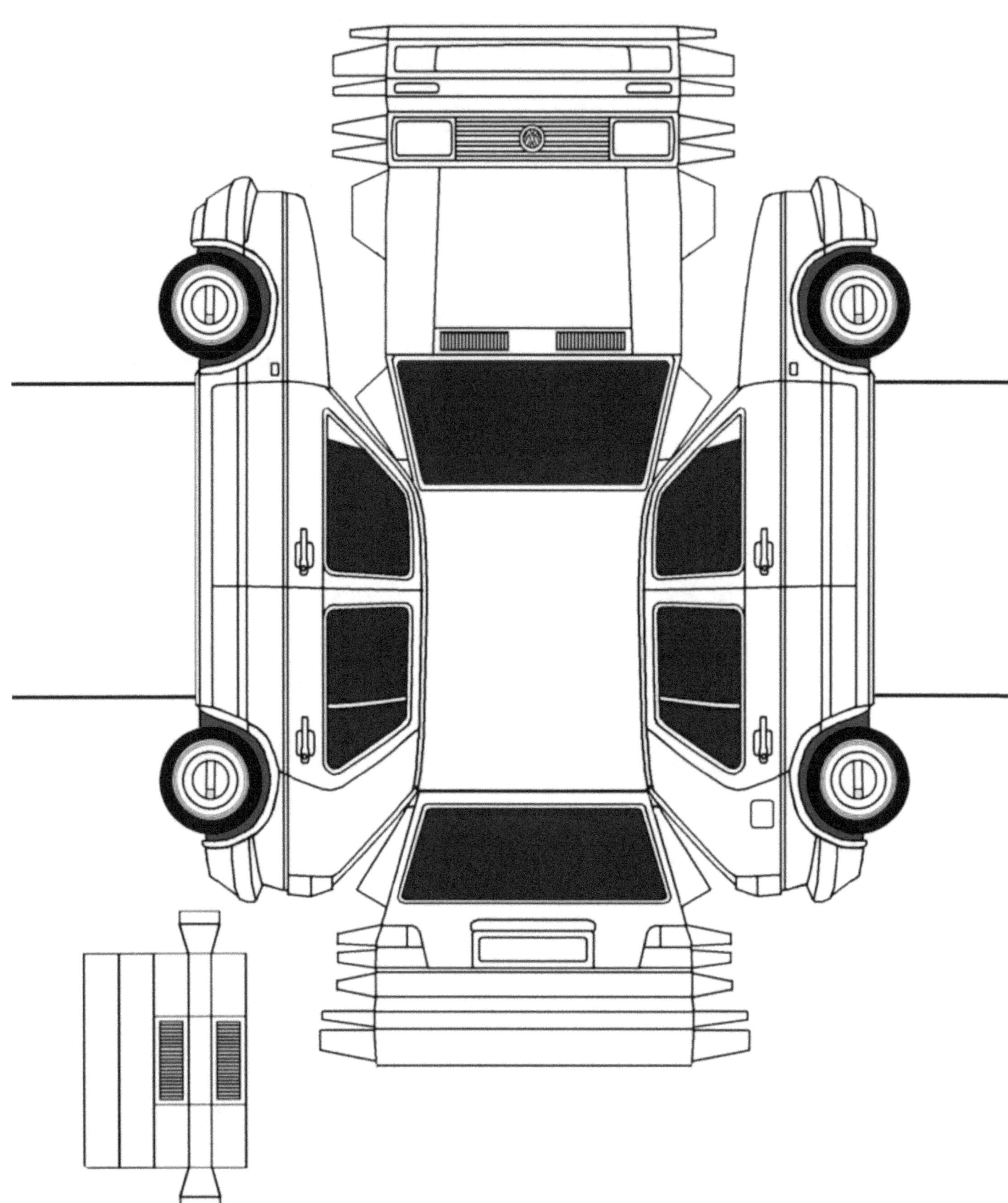

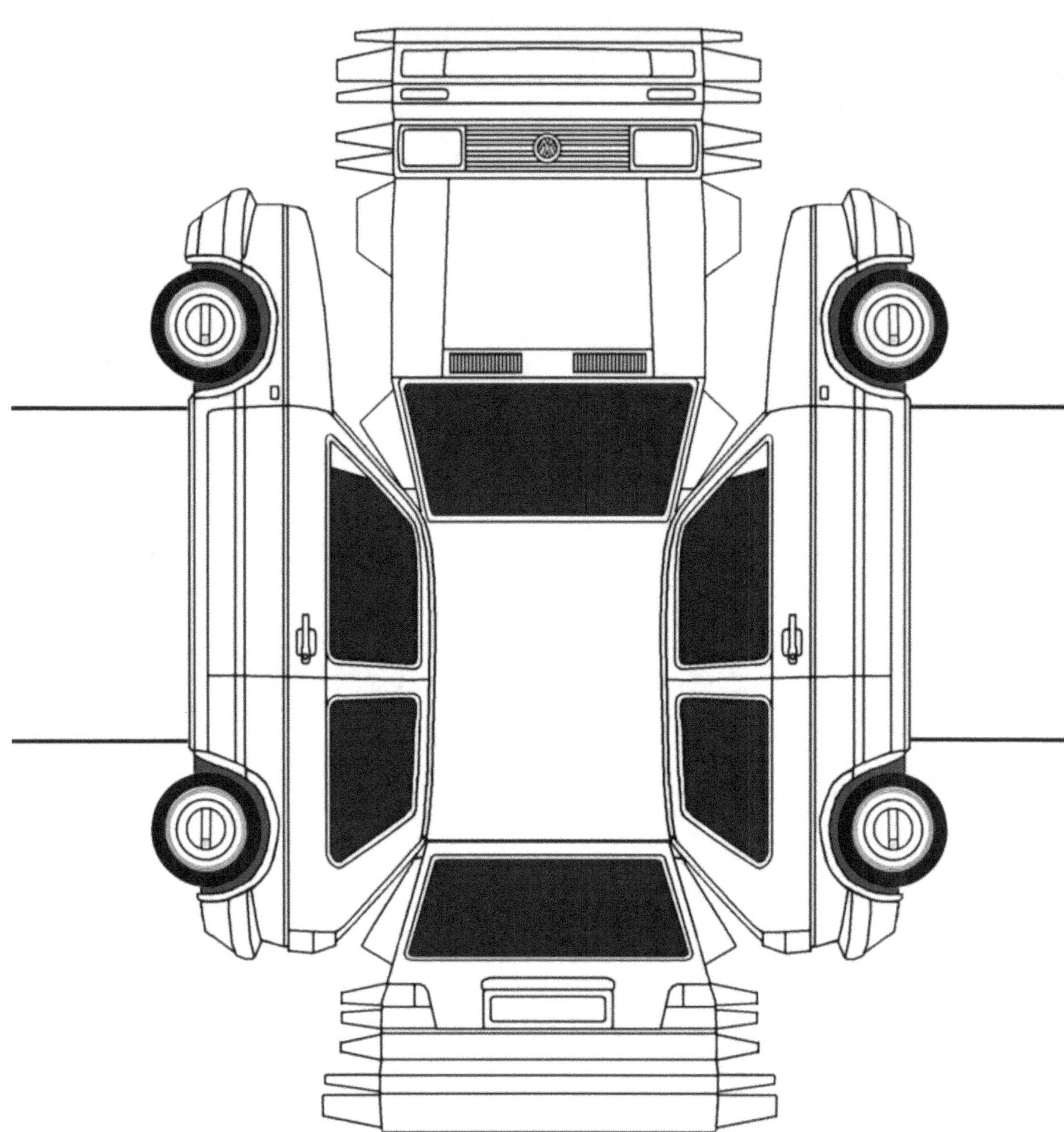

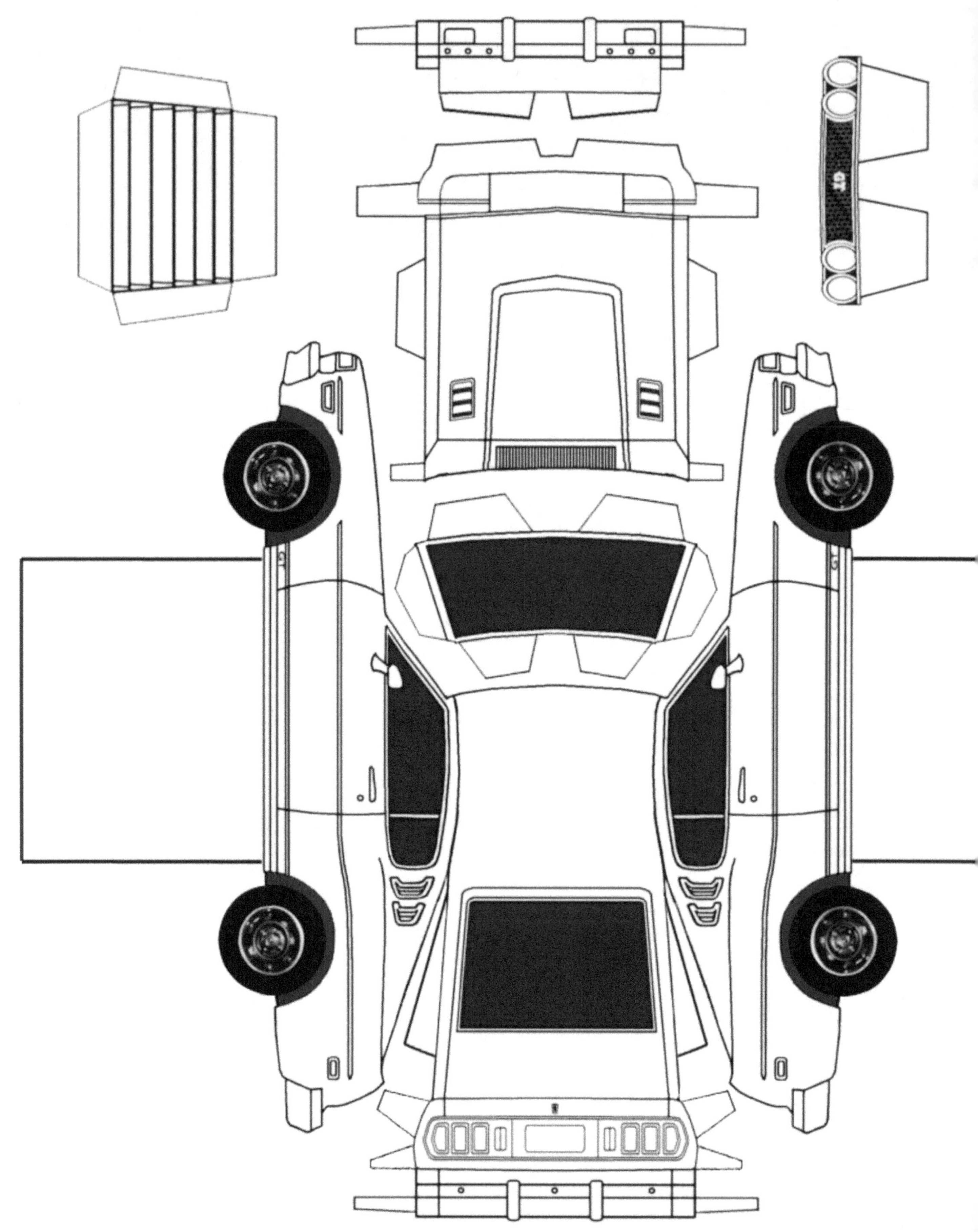

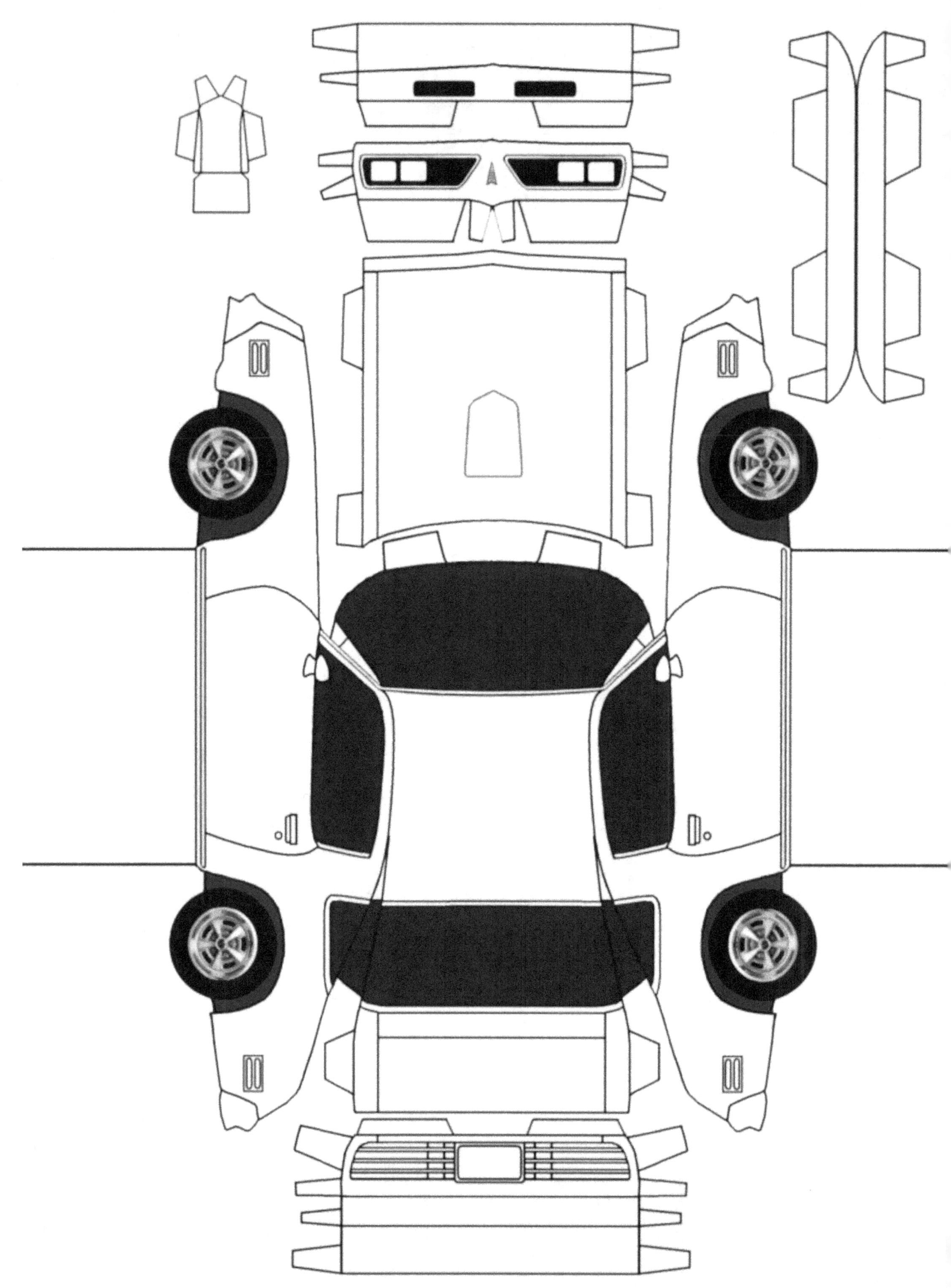

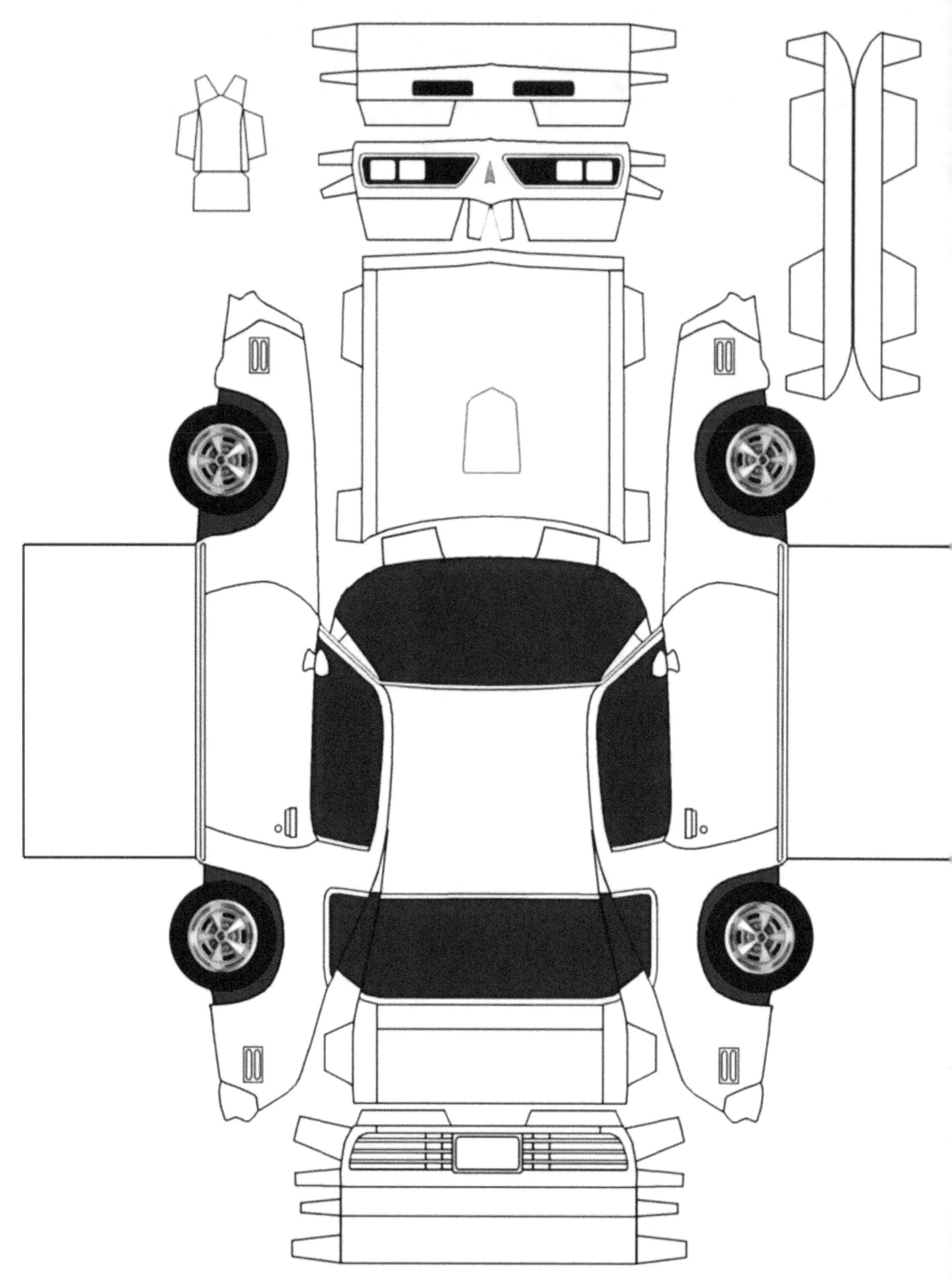

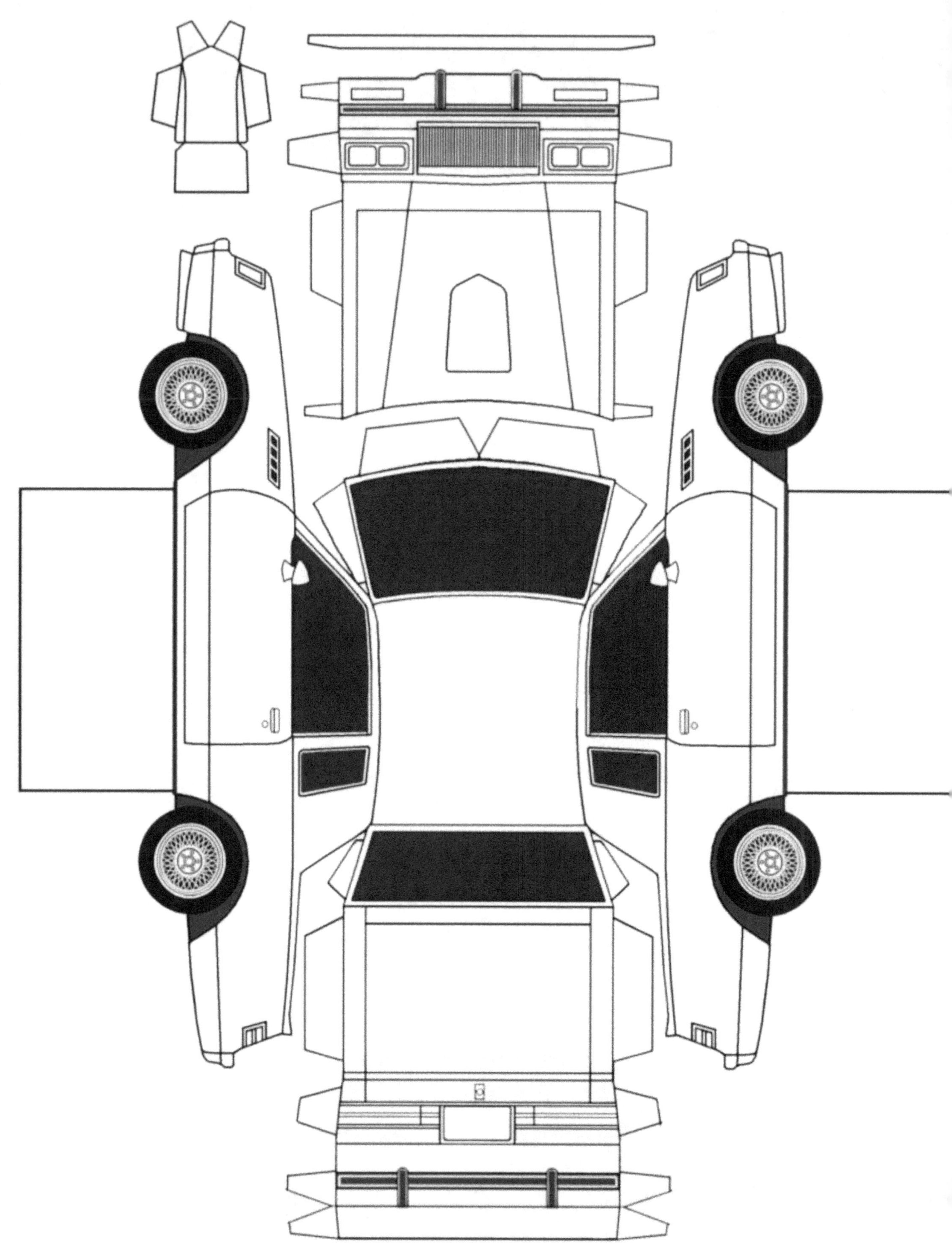

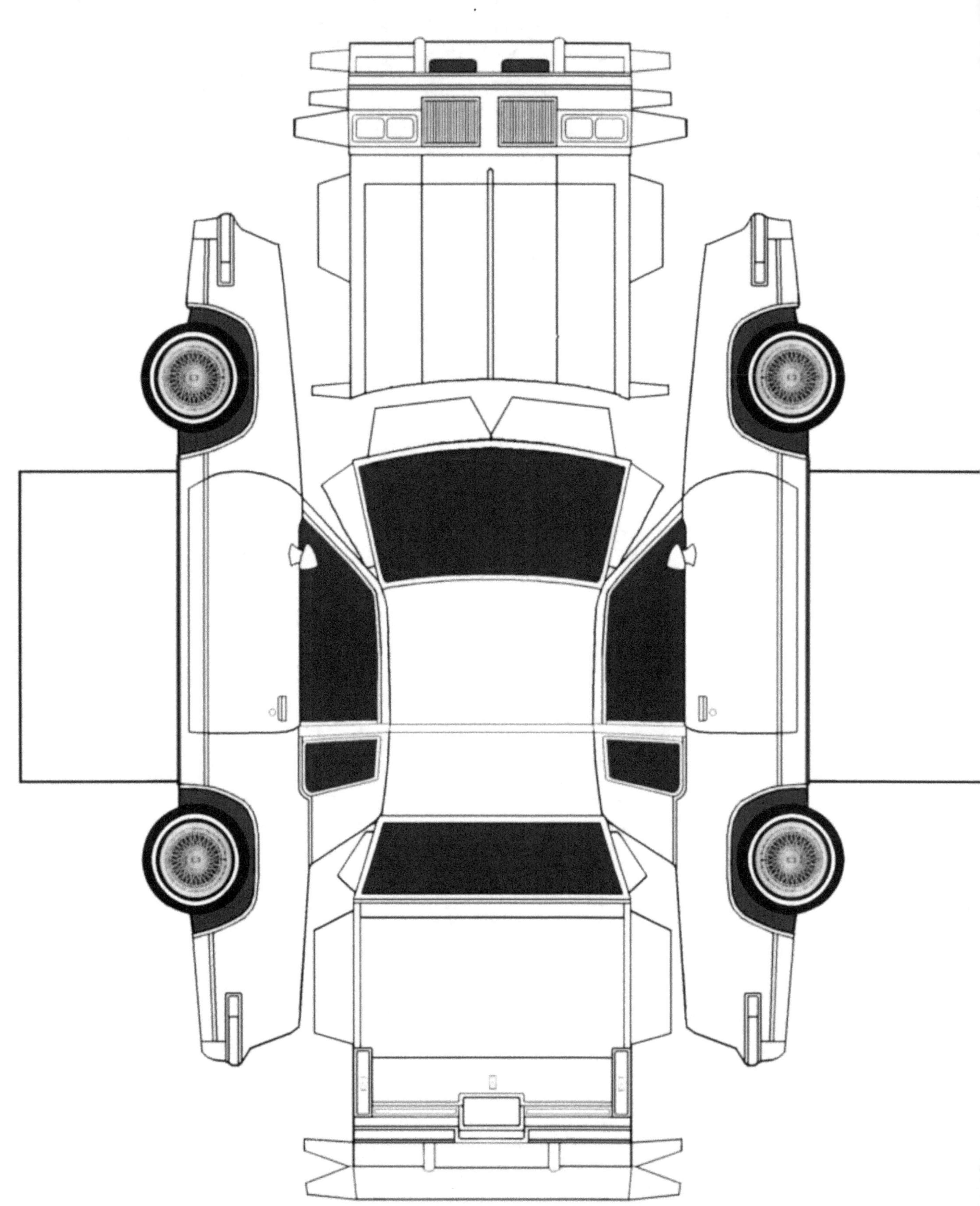

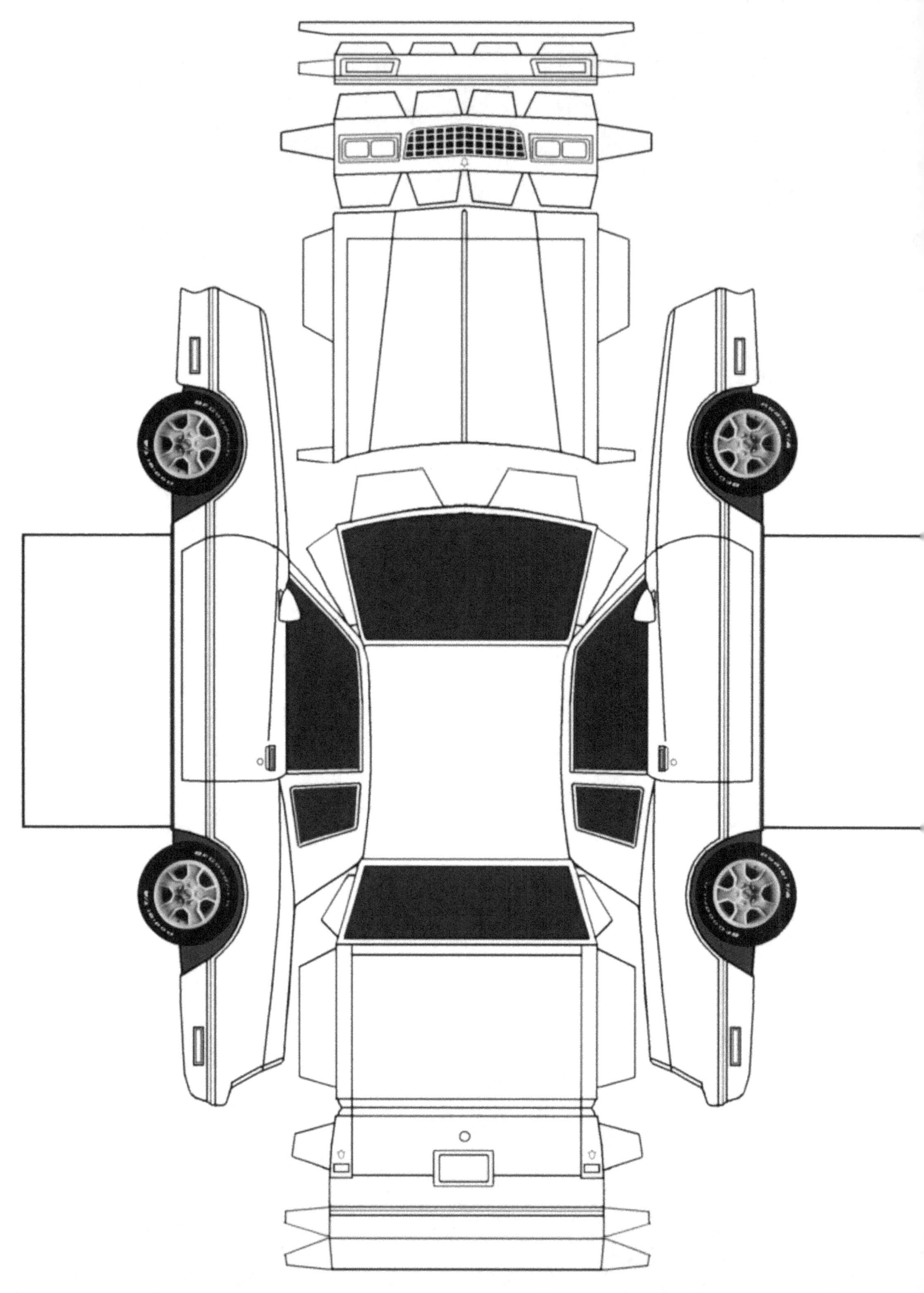

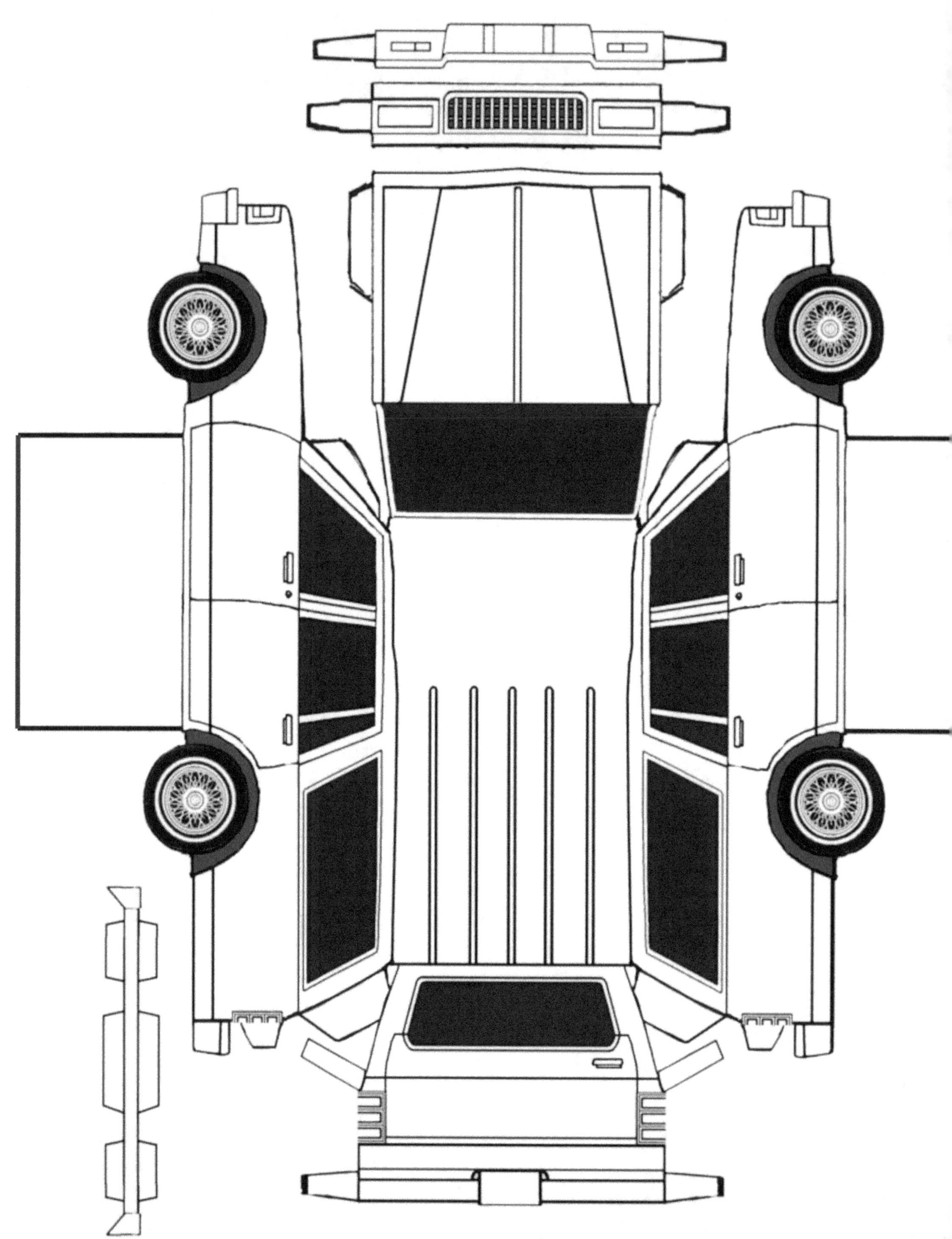

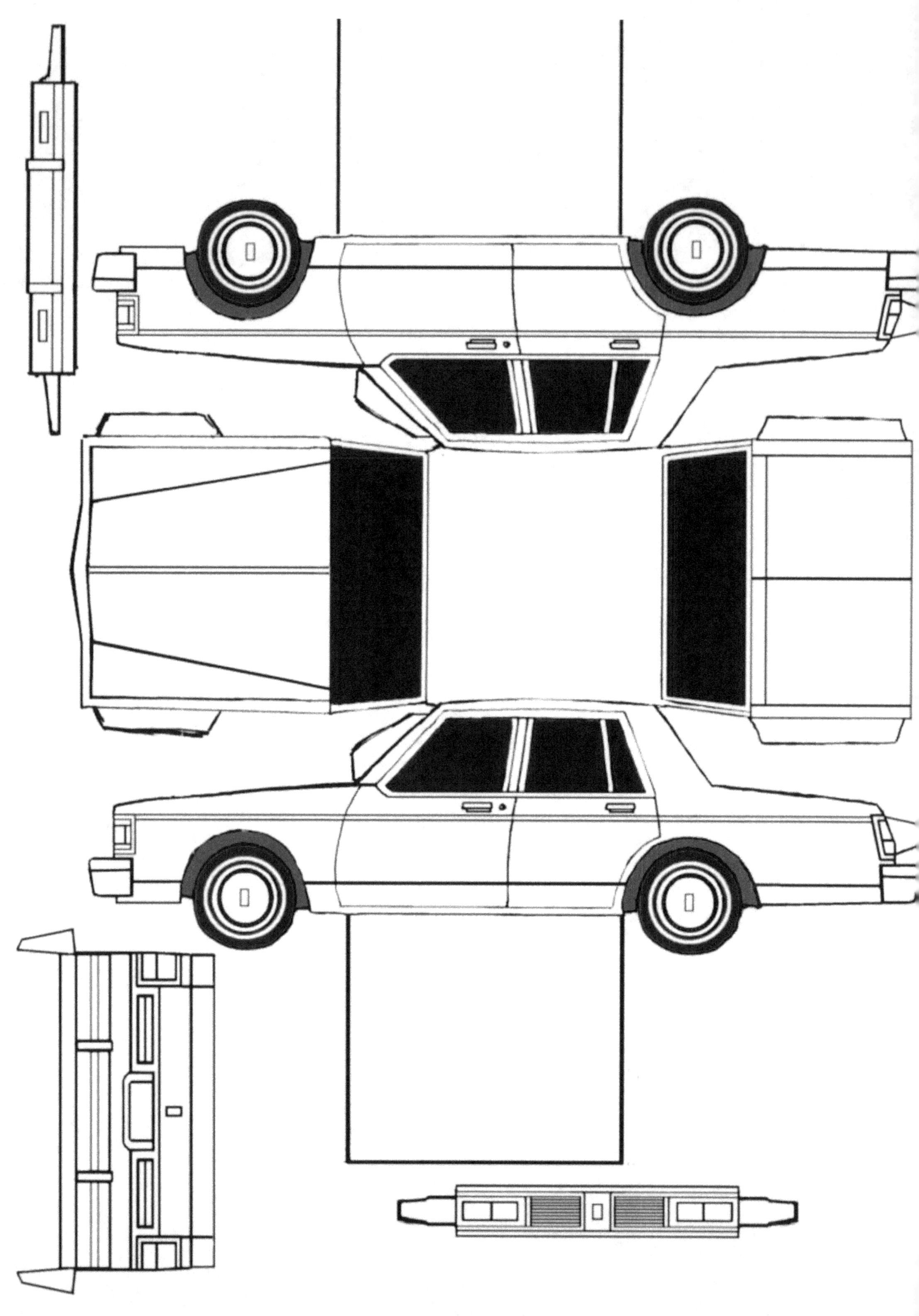

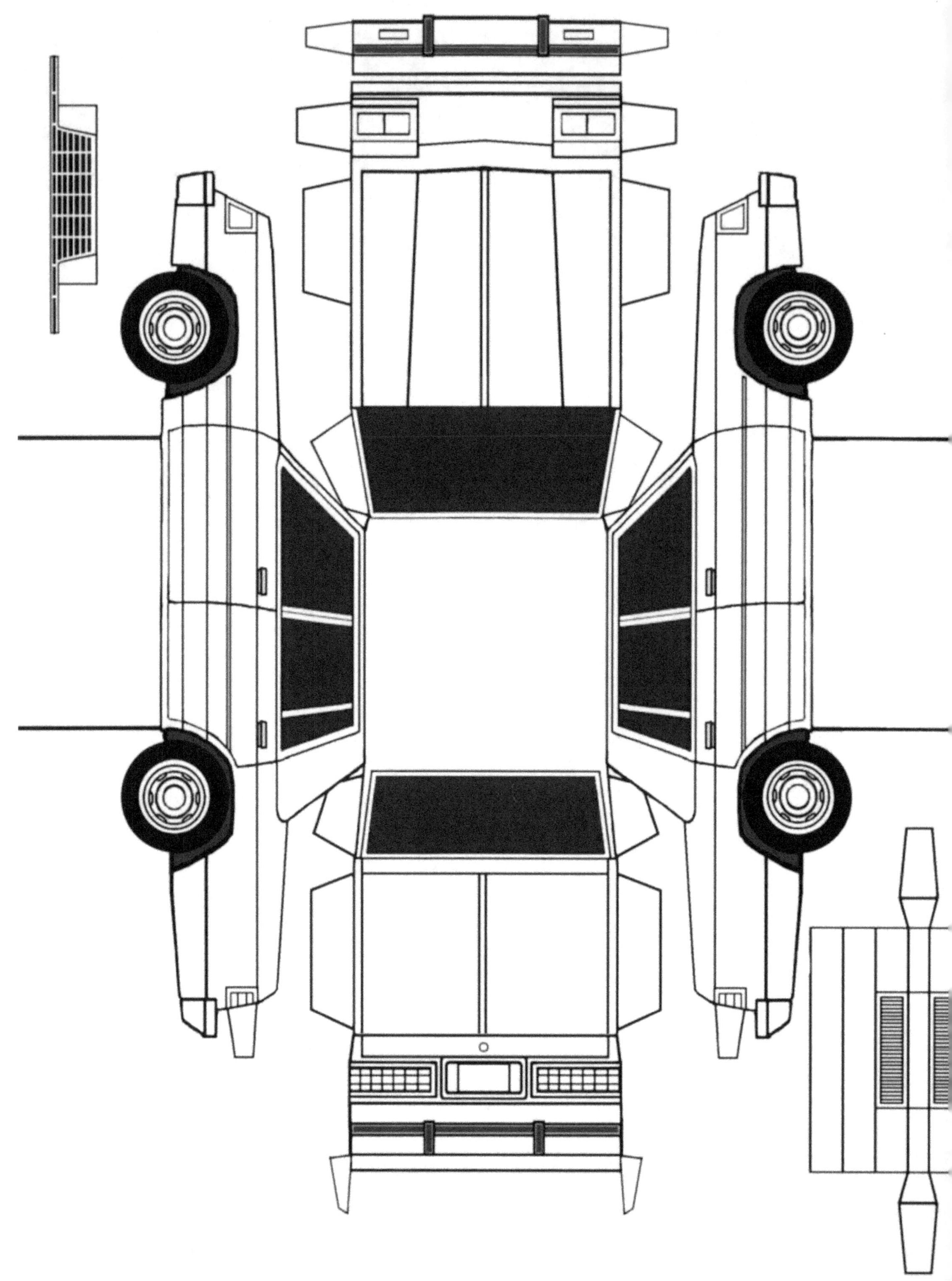

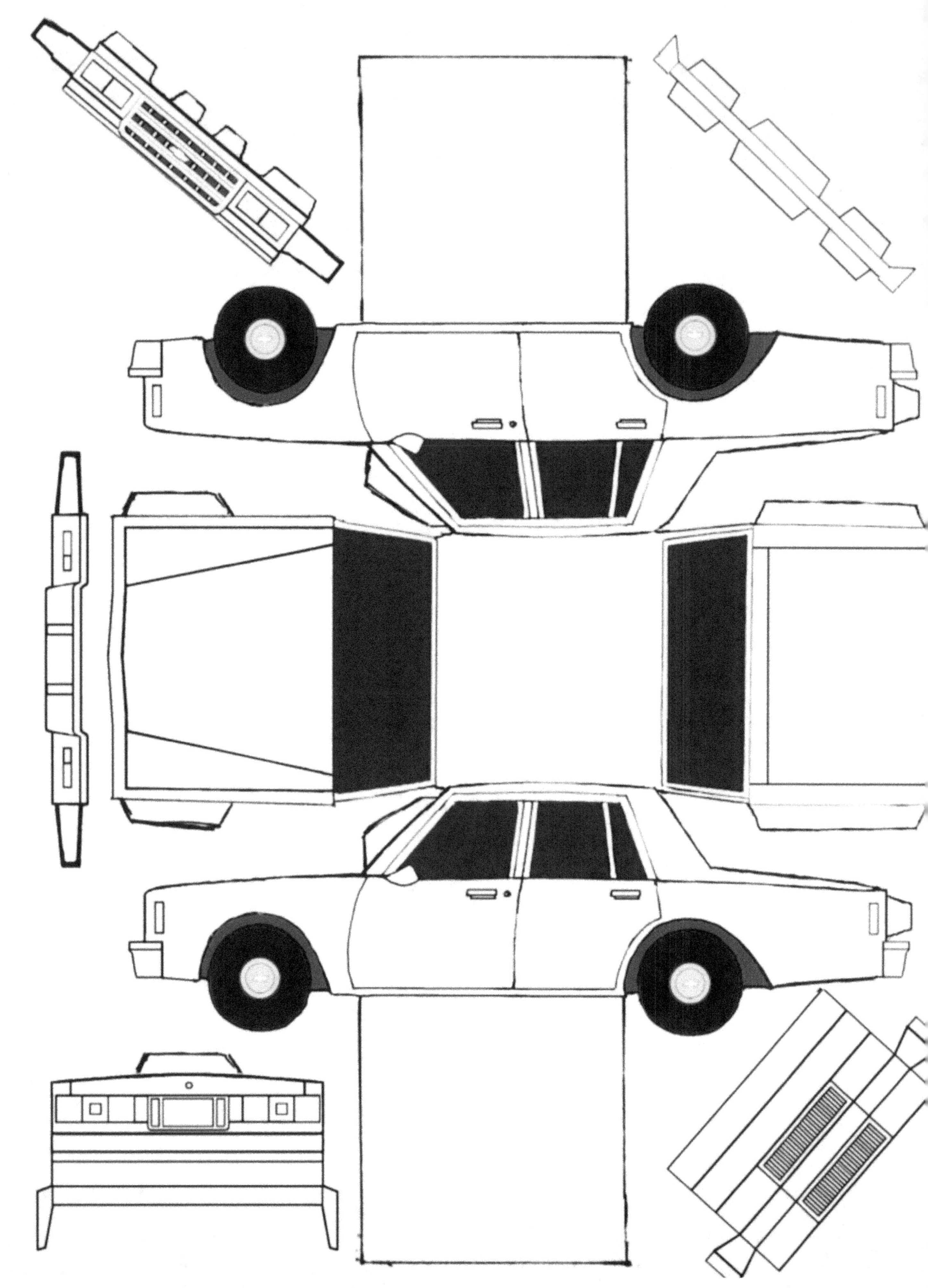

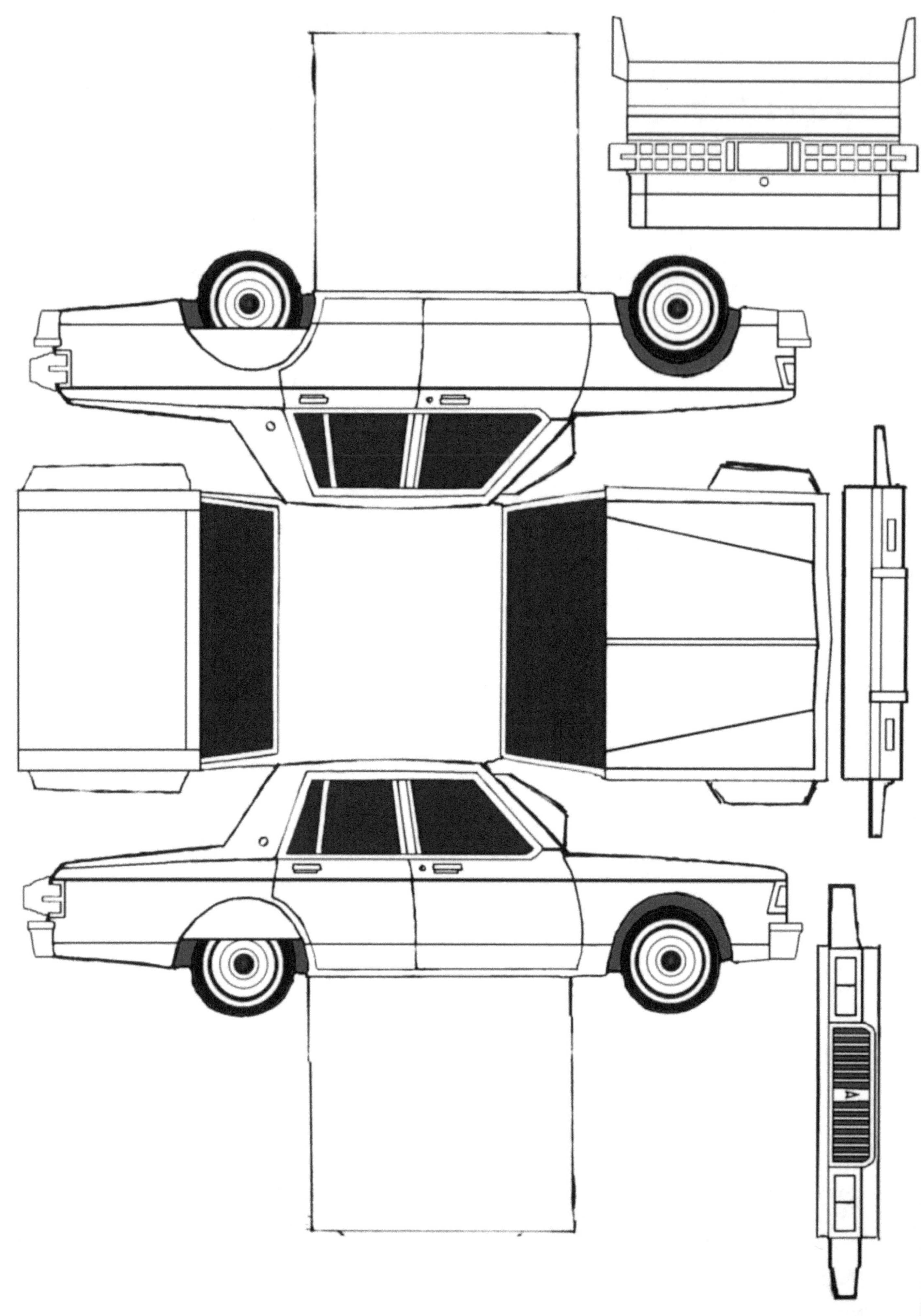

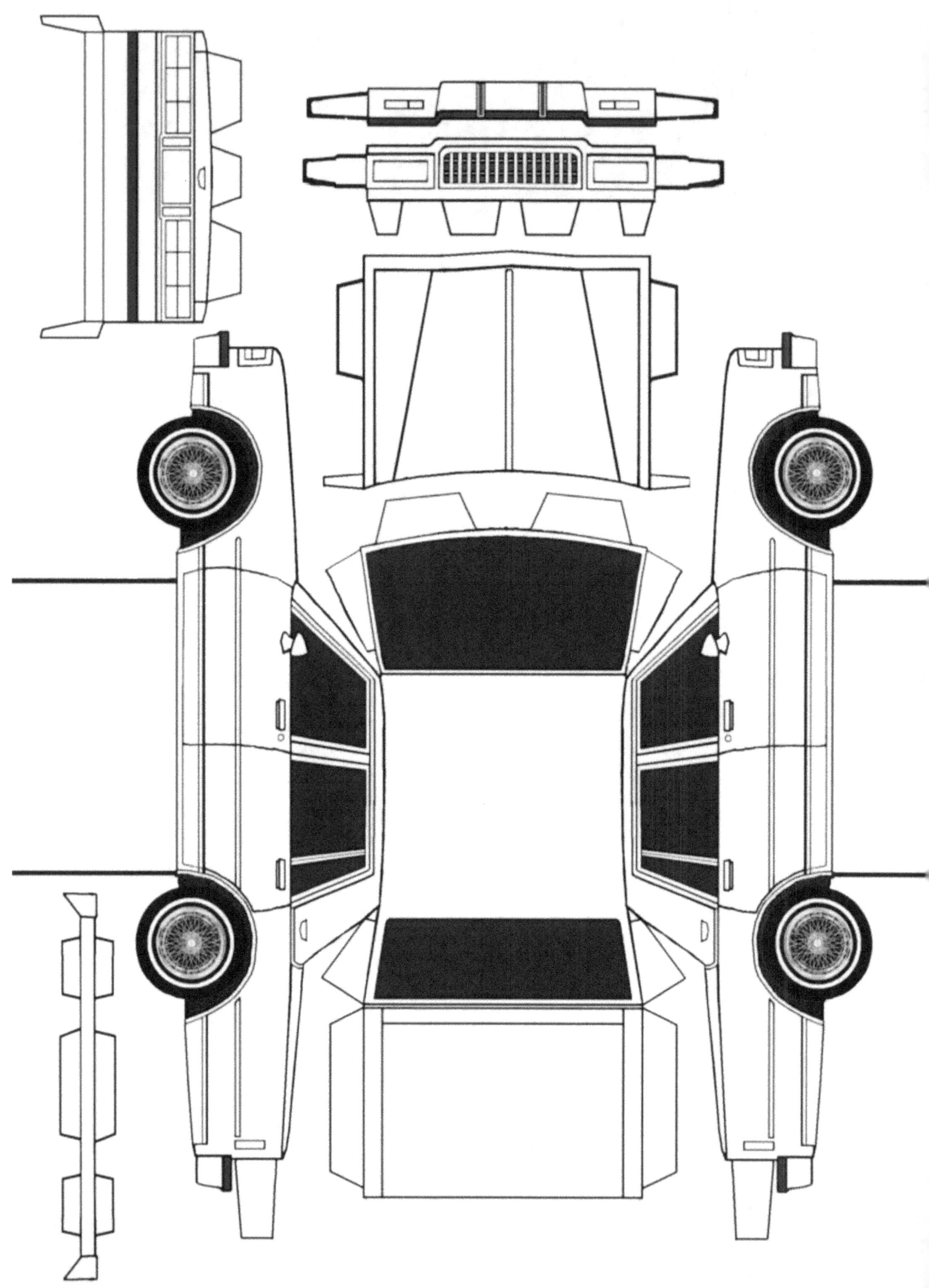

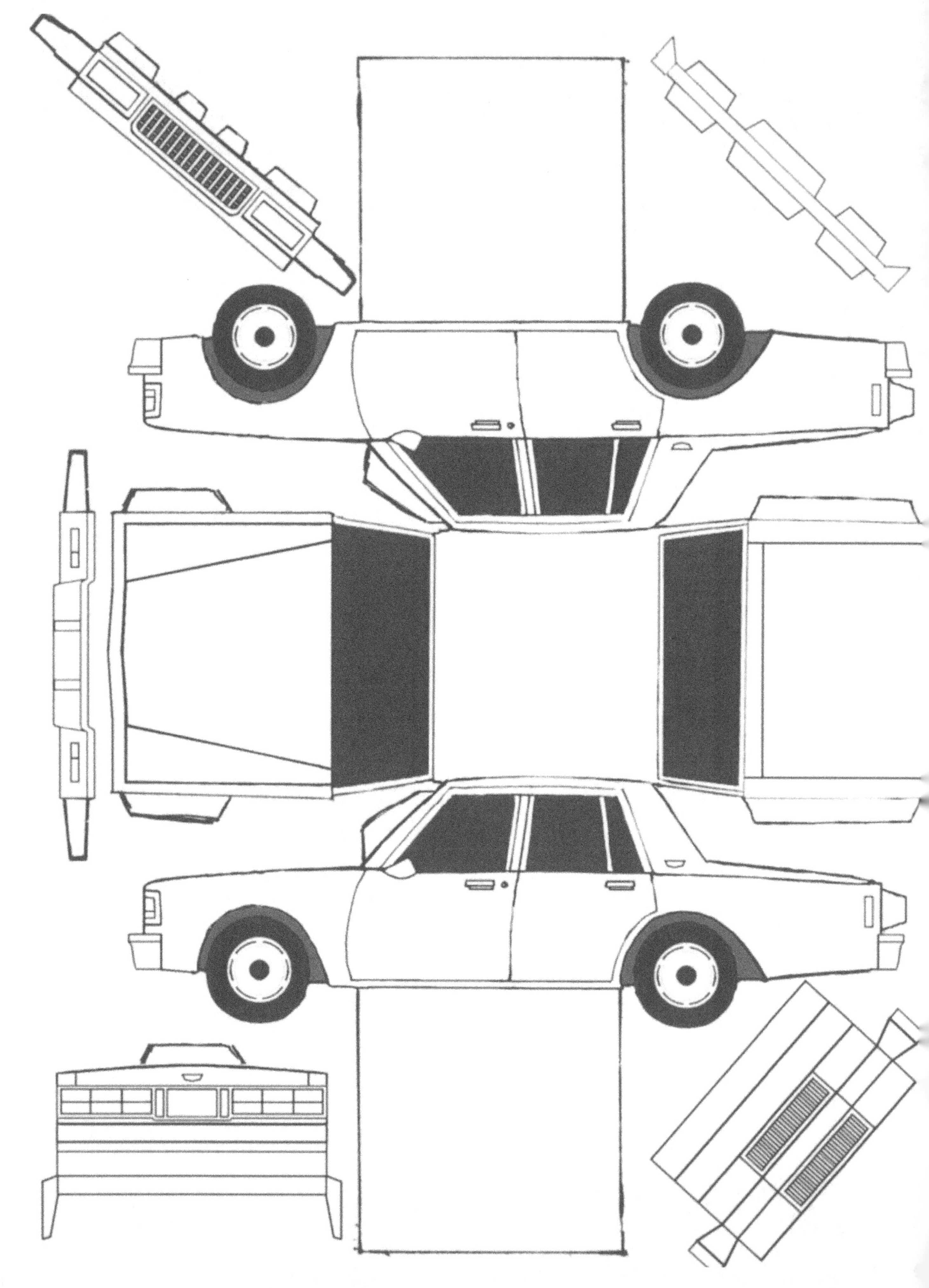

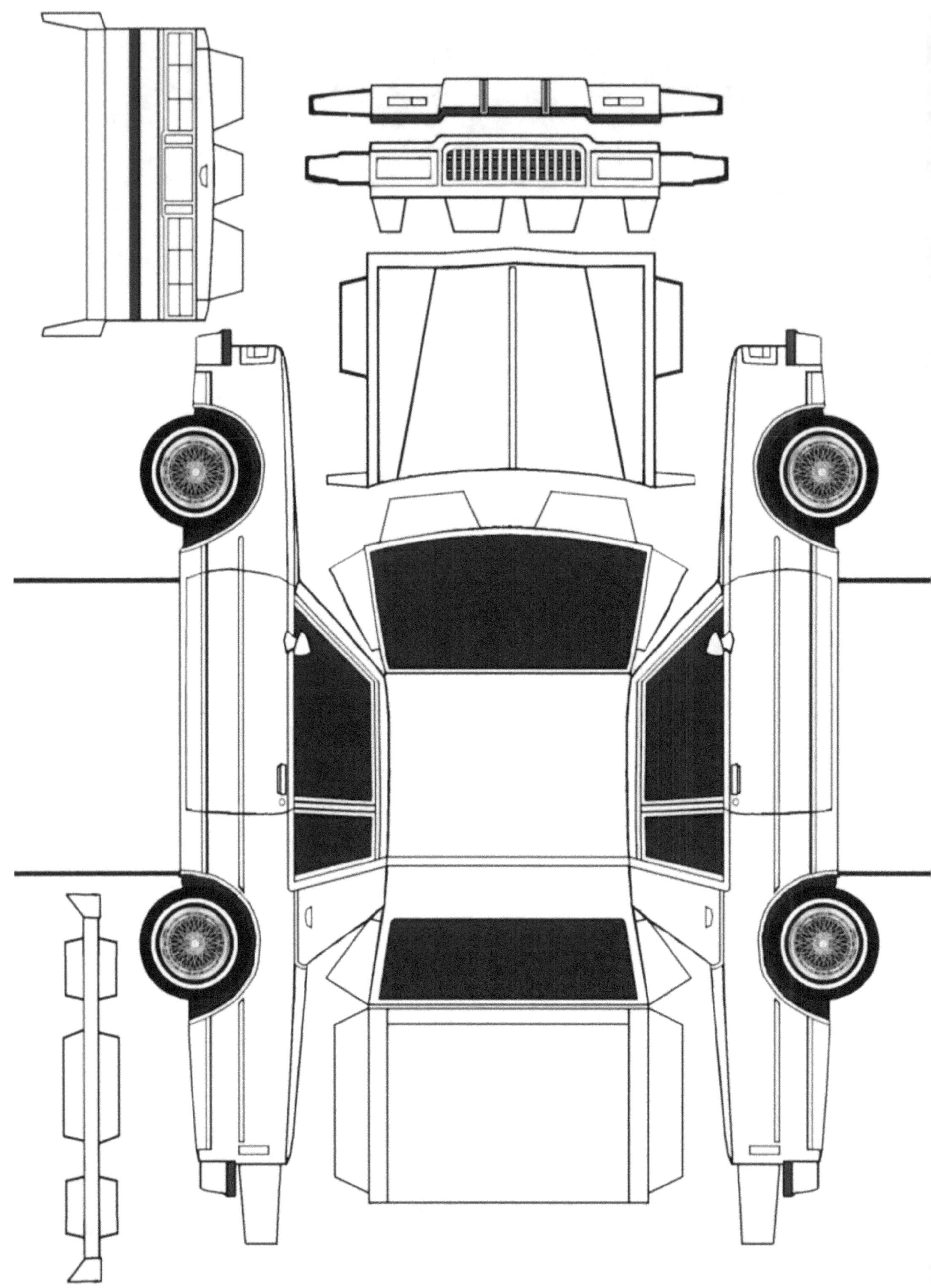

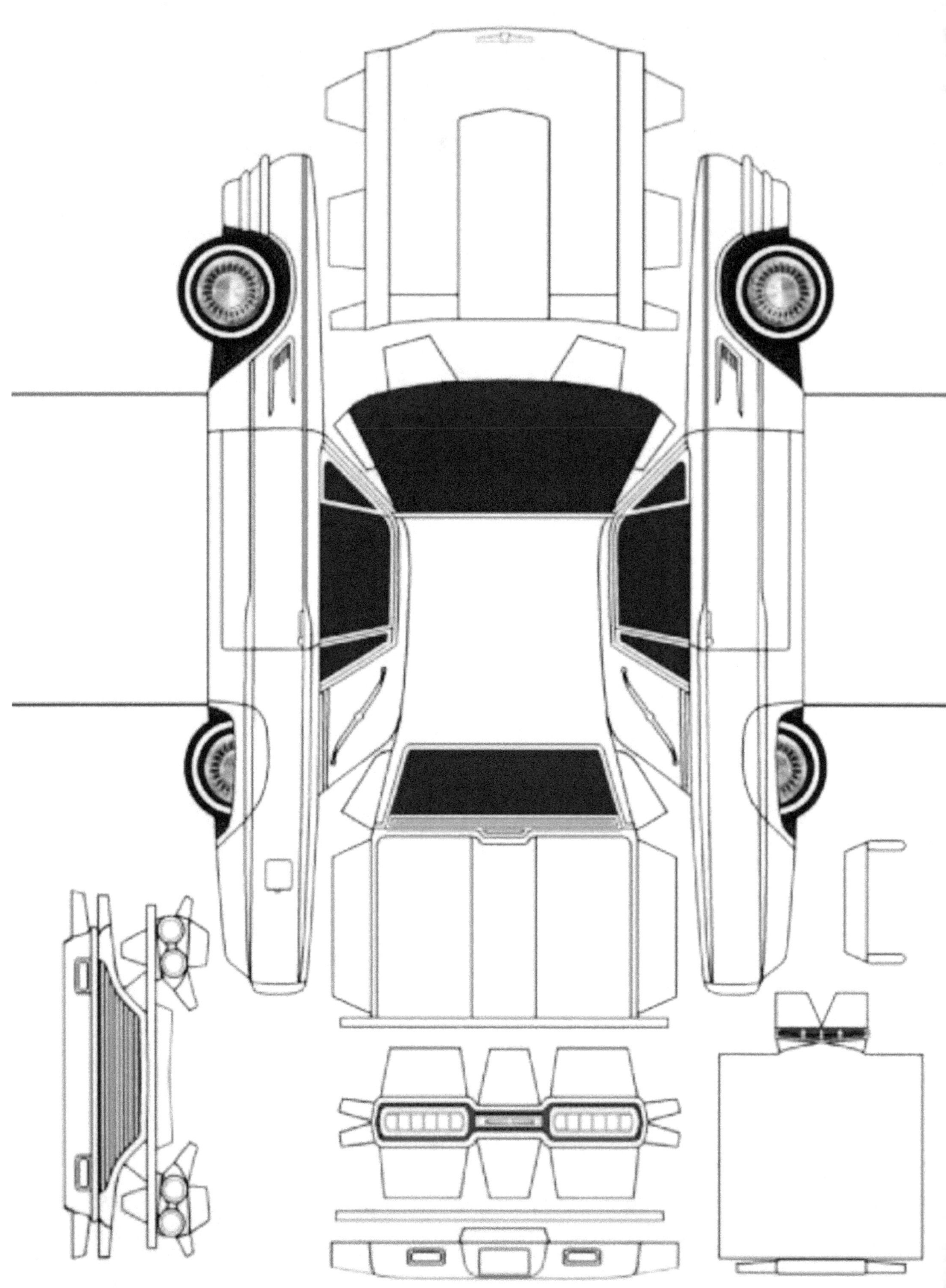

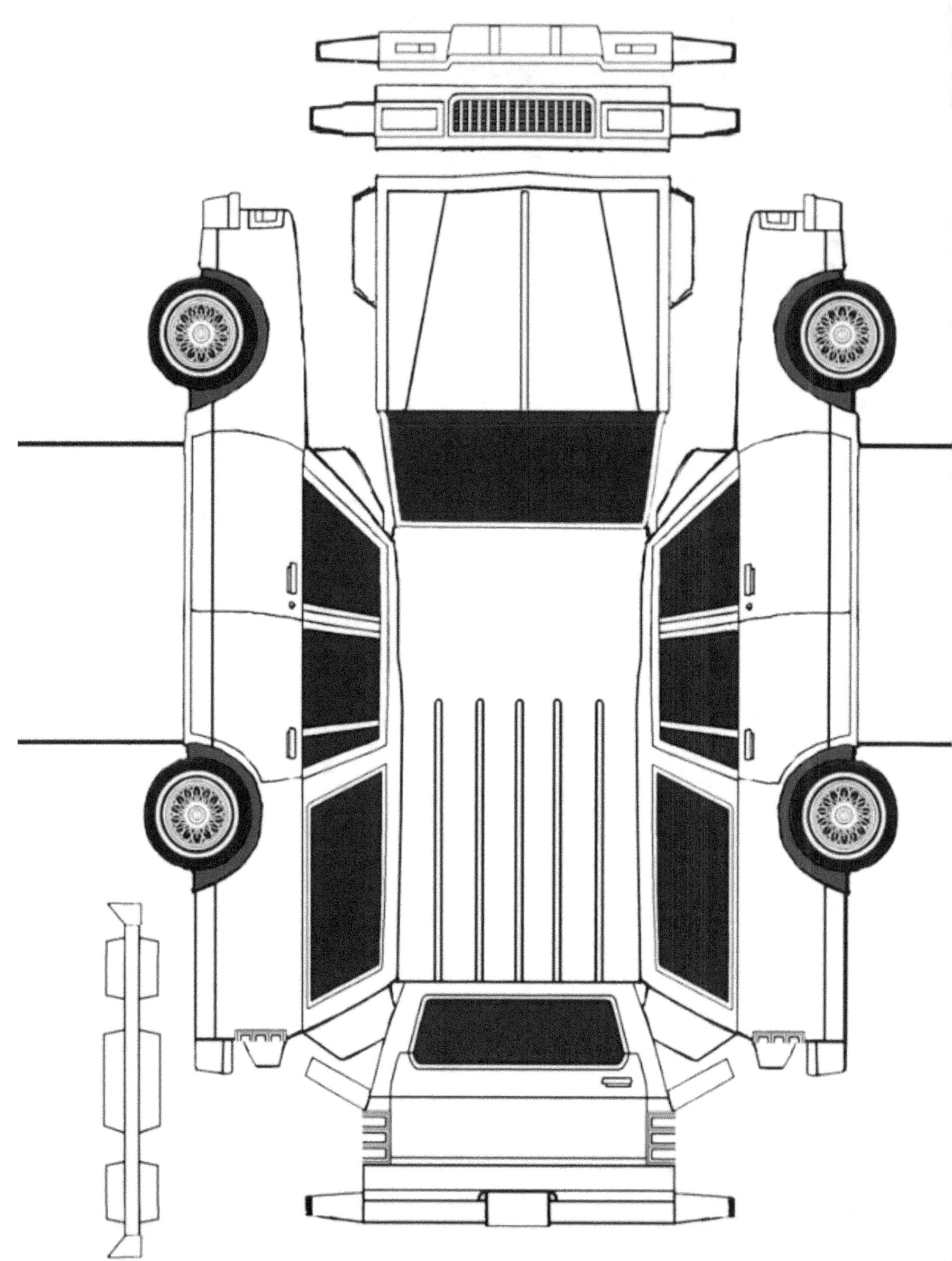

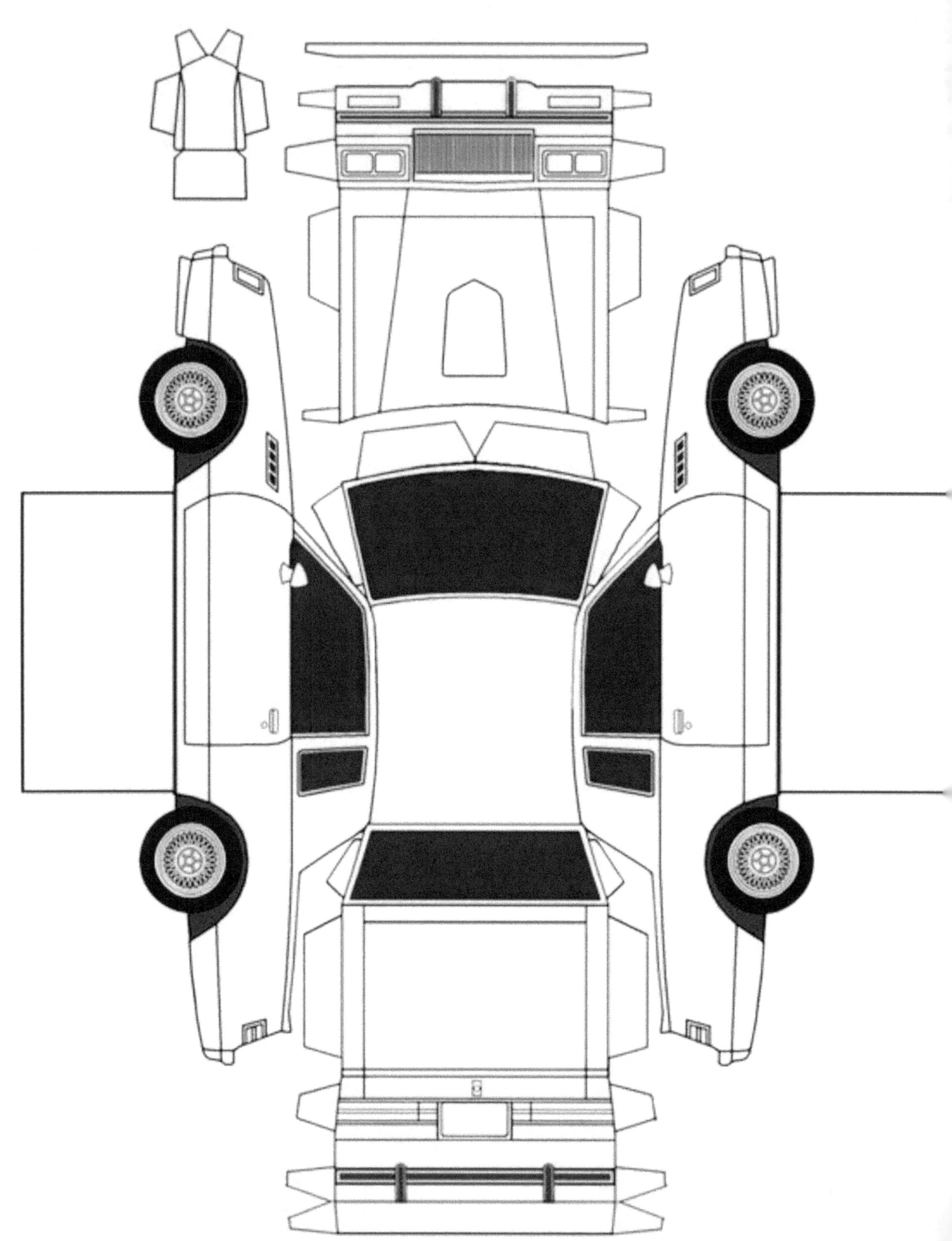

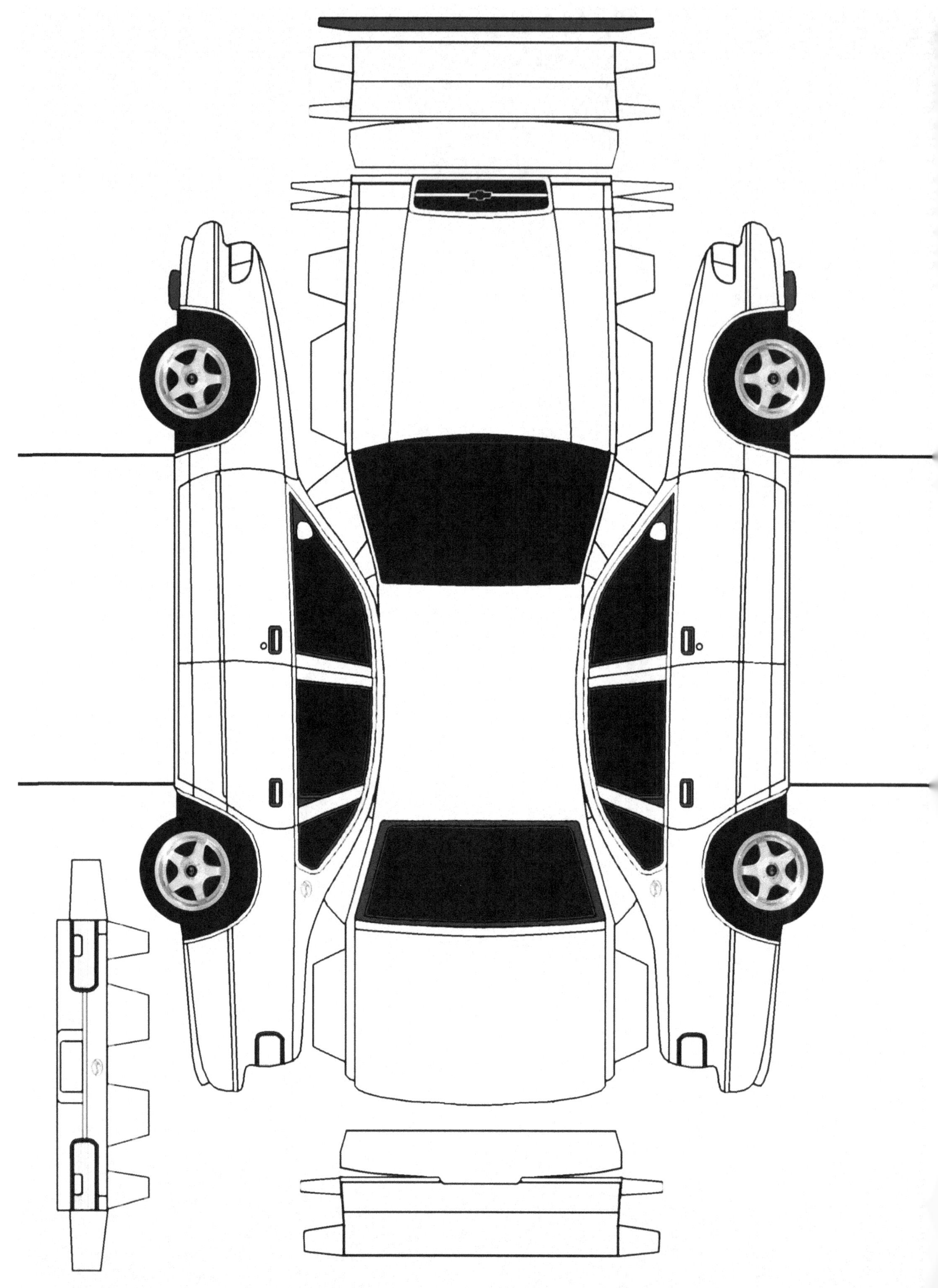

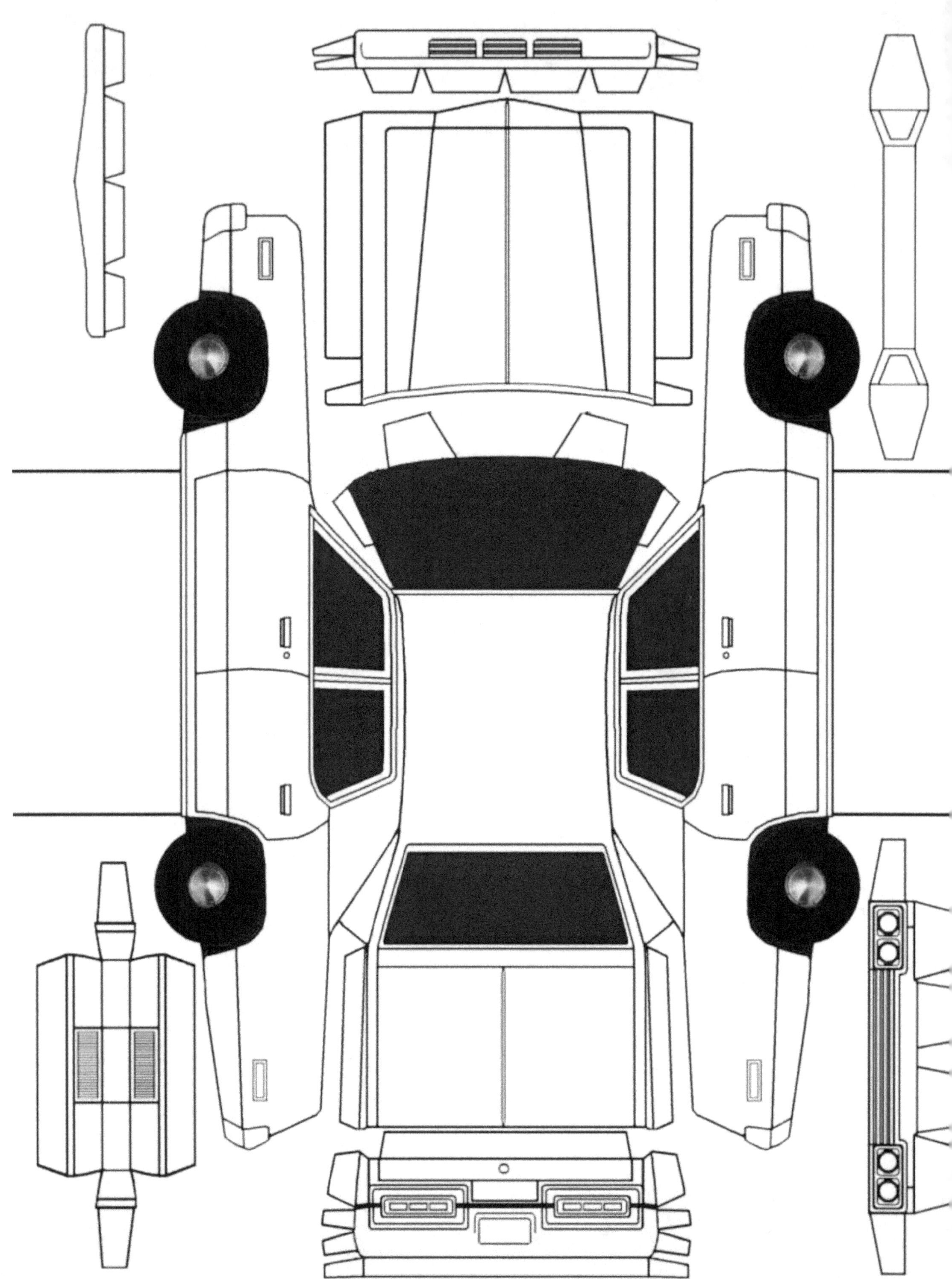

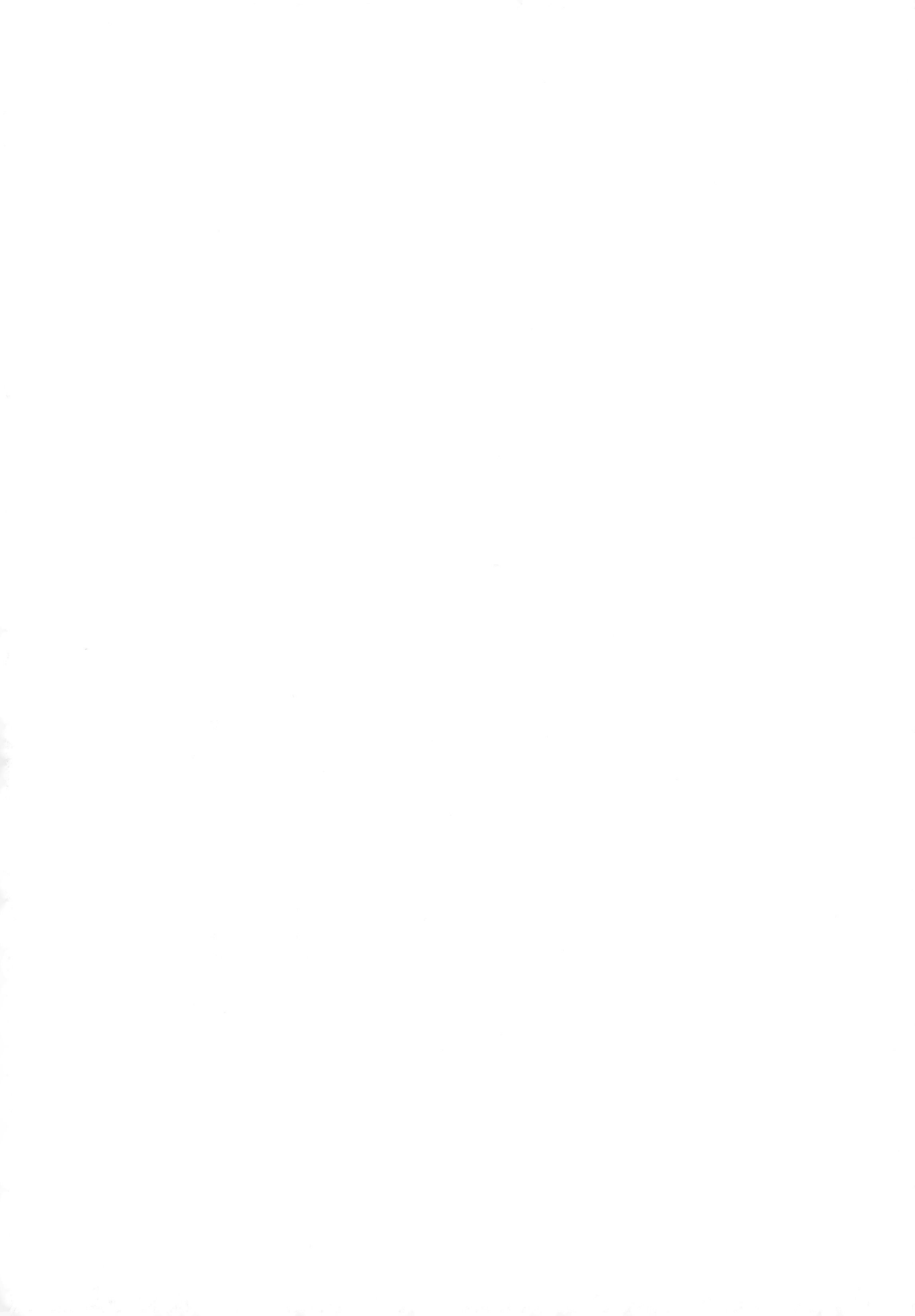

www.ingramcontent.com/pod-product-compliance
Lightning Source LLC
Chambersburg PA
CBHW082344270726
48658CB00017B/3116